Cambridge Elements

Elements in Soviet and Post-Soviet History
edited by
Mark Edele
University of Melbourne
Rebecca Friedman
Florida International University

THE IRON CURTAIN

A Short History of Socialist Borders

Lorenz M. Lüthi
McGill University

CAMBRIDGE
UNIVERSITY PRESS

Shaftesbury Road, Cambridge CB2 8EA, United Kingdom

One Liberty Plaza, 20th Floor, New York, NY 10006, USA

477 Williamstown Road, Port Melbourne, VIC 3207, Australia

314–321, 3rd Floor, Plot 3, Splendor Forum, Jasola District Centre,
New Delhi – 110025, India

Cambridge University Press is part of Cambridge University Press & Assessment,
a department of the University of Cambridge.

We share the University's mission to contribute to society through the pursuit of
education, learning and research at the highest international levels of excellence.

www.cambridge.org
Information on this title: www.cambridge.org/9781009712781

DOI: 10.1017/9781009712811

© Lorenz M. Lüthi 2026

This publication is in copyright. Subject to statutory exception and to the provisions
of relevant collective licensing agreements, no reproduction of any part may take
place without the written permission of Cambridge University Press & Assessment.

When citing this work, please include a reference to the DOI 10.1017/9781009712811

First published 2026

A catalogue record for this publication is available from the British Library

*A Cataloging-in-Publication data record for this Element is available from the
Library of Congress*

ISBN 978-1-009-71278-1 Hardback
ISBN 978-1-009-71277-4 Paperback
ISSN 2753-5290 (online)
ISSN 2753-5282 (print)

Cambridge University Press & Assessment has no responsibility for the persistence
or accuracy of URLs for external or third-party internet websites referred to in this
publication and does not guarantee that any content on such websites is, or will remain,
accurate or appropriate.

For EU product safety concerns, contact us at Calle de José Abascal, 56, 1°, 28003
Madrid, Spain, or email eugpsr@cambridge.org

The Iron Curtain

A Short History of Socialist Borders

Elements in Soviet and Post-Soviet History

DOI: 10.1017/9781009712811
First published online: March 2026

Lorenz M. Lüthi
McGill University

Author for correspondence: Lorenz M. Lüthi, lorenz.luthi@mcgill.ca

Abstract: The Iron Curtain remains an iconic representation of the Cold War. But what was it really on the ground? Fortified borders to prevent citizens from leaving emerged first in the interwar USSR and then in socialist post–World War II Europe. Fortifications occurred both at borders between socialist states and at their external boundaries to the non-socialist world, but not in all cases. The most well-known case – the Berlin Wall – was both an extreme example and a latecomer. But since 1947, Yugoslavia, Hungary, and Czechoslovakia had fortified their borders to prevent exit. When East Germany started to build walls around West Berlin and at its borders to West Germany in the 1960s, Yugoslavia was already dismantling its border regime and Hungary was granting passports and exit visas to its citizens. Fortified borders also appeared at external borders in Northern and Southeastern Europe, in the Caucasus, and in Asia.

Keywords: Cold War, borders, socialist world, USSR, East Germany

© Lorenz M. Lüthi 2026

ISBNs: 9781009712781 (HB), 9781009712774 (PB), 9781009712811 (OC)
ISSNs: 2753-5290 (online), 2753-5282 (print)

Contents

	Introduction	1
1	Soviet Interwar Borders	6
2	*Churchill's Iron Curtain* in East Europe	12
3	Yugoslavia's Iron Curtains, 1945–1965	17
4	Hungary's Iron Curtain, 1945–1955	24
5	Czechoslovakia's Iron Curtain, 1945–1955	28
6	East Germany's Iron Curtain, 1945–1955	34
7	Czechoslovakia's and Hungary's Divergent Border Regimes, 1955–1989	42
8	East Germany's Walls	50
9	Other Iron Curtains	59
	Conclusions	70
	Primary Sources Used	73
	Note on Terminology	75
	Further Readings	76

Introduction

"From Stettin in the Baltic to Trieste in the Adriatic, an iron curtain has descended across the continent. Behind that line lie all the capitals of the ancient states of central and eastern Europe. Warsaw, Berlin, Prague, Vienna, Budapest, Belgrade, Bucharest, and Sofia, ..., " declared former British Prime Minister Winston Churchill in Fulton, Missouri, on March 5, 1946. Five days later, the *New York Times* explained what Churchill had meant, providing a map of Europe that exhibited a wall running down from the Baltic coast west of Szczecin/Stettin, along the Oder-Neisse-river system, the western borders of Czechoslovakia and Hungary, and then the northwestern border of Yugoslavia to the Adriatic coast just east of Trieste (Map 1).[1] But both Churchill and the *New York Times* had overstated the case. Neither did an Iron Curtain that hermetically sealed Eastern from Western Europe exist in the spring of 1946, nor was Berlin behind it. Millions of ethnic Germans, East European Jews, and displaced persons of many nationalities moved across this line in either direction for years after World War II. And no *wall* ever graced that particular line, although concrete walls divided Germany and enclosed West Berlin after 1961.

Within ten days, Joseph Stalin claimed that Churchill had borrowed the term Iron Curtain from "Hitler and his friends."[2] He, too, overstated his case. The term originated in the late eighteenth century and denoted a theater's metal fire curtain that could be lowered to separate the stage hermetically from the audience in the fire-prone theaters of the time. In World War I, it also assumed the political meaning of hermetically sealing borders between two states. Almost a decade after the war, a German politician bemoaned the "iron curtain" that had separated France and Germany politically and economically since World War I.[3] Moreover, since the October Revolution in 1917, Western politicians and journalists had used the metaphor to describe the increasing self-isolation of Soviet Russia (since 1922, the Union of Socialist Soviet Republics/ USSR). The term reappeared after World War II in descriptions of Soviet foreign policy in Europe. Churchill himself used the term in June of 1945 in a telegram to US President Harry S. Truman, and again in August at the opening of the new House of Commons.[4] In short, in March 1946, he merely turned a widely used trope into an iconic Cold War metaphor.

---

[1] *NYT*, 3/6/1946:4 (quote); *NYT*, 3/10/1946:E5.
[2] "Interview of Comrade I.V. Stalin with a 'Pravda' correspondent on Churchill's Speech," *Pravda*, 3/14/1946, p. 1.
[3] Christian Koller, "Der Eiserne Vorhang," *Zeitschrift für Geschichtswissenschaft*, 54/4 (2006), pp. 372–73; *NZZ*-n, 9/30/1919:1; *NZZ*-e, 2/6/1928:1 (quote).
[4] Koller, "Der Eiserne Vorhang," p. 375; "The British Prime Minister (Churchill) to President Truman," 6/4/1945, United States, Department of State, *Foreign Relations of the United States*, vol. III (U.S. Government Printing Office, 1968), p. 326; *Newsweek*, 8/27/1945:44.

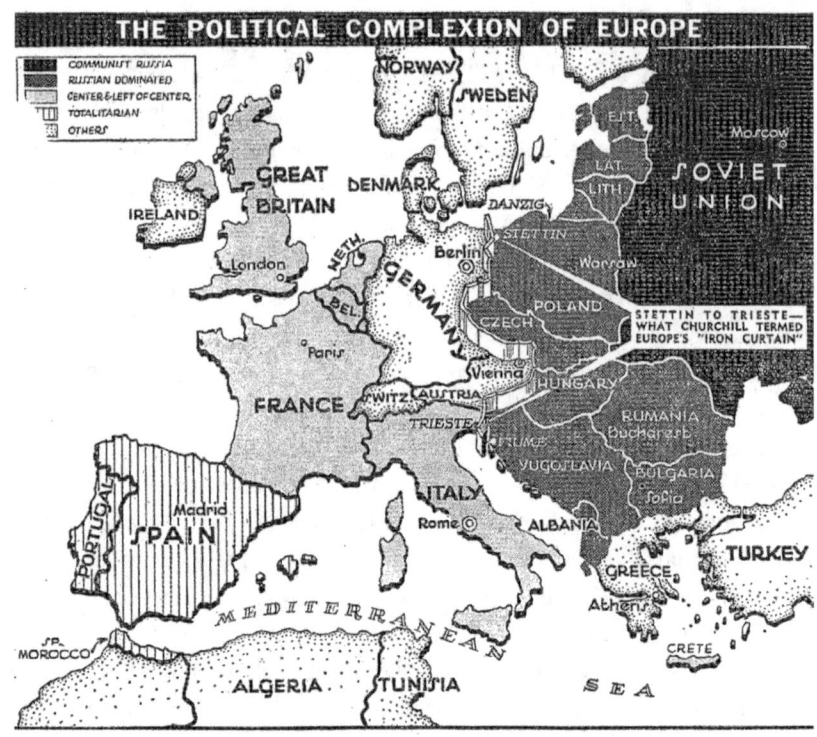

Map 1 Five days after Churchill's famous speech, the *New York Times* published this map, showing a wall where none ever existed.
Source: *NYT*, March 10, 1946, p. E5.

But how did the Iron Curtain look like on the ground during the Cold War? The various forms of Iron Curtains call for a historical analysis that decenters the Cold War by focusing on national borders of the Socialist Camp instead of concentrating exclusively on Soviet border policies and fortifications. In any case, the term "Iron Curtain" usually brings to our mind pictures of the so-called Berlin Wall between 1961 and 1989. Historically, the Iron Curtain around West Berlin and its concurrent counterpart along the German–German border were just the most extreme examples of external borders of the Socialist Camp. Both initially consisted of barbed wire and brick stone barriers. Only with time, they became concrete walls – flanked by a death strip with mines, ditches, barbed wires, electrified fences, and fast-shooting guards – that ripped apart the German capital and even German villages from 1961 to 1989. The *primary* purpose of the German Iron Curtain was to prevent East German citizens from leaving because the communist regime needed their labor to build up a socialist state. Unsurprisingly, the Berlin and German walls became places of spectacular escapes. Trains and armored cars broke through, small airplanes and balloons crossed above, tunnels traversed underground, and people managed to pass across. But refugees were also stopped, arrested, and killed.[5] Between October 1949 and November 1989, at least 159 refugees were killed at the borders around West Berlin and at least 327 at the German–German border.[6]

Yet, the walls dividing Berlin and Germany were not only *extreme* cases, but also *late* developments at the Iron Curtain between the Baltic and the Adriatic Sea. The western borders of Hungary and Czechoslovakia had been fortified with barbed wire, minefields, and shooting border guards – but not walls – as early as the end of the 1940s to prevent people from leaving. Interestingly, Hungary started to reduce its border regime in the second half of the 1960s, when East Germany was building walls around West Berlin and through Germany. East Germany and Czechoslovakia recurrently shot and killed fleeing citizens until 1989, while Hungary's western border became remarkably, but not completely, non-lethal for the last two decades of the Cold War. Nevertheless, the very last illegal border crosser of the Central European Iron Curtain – a citizen of the GDR – was shot dead at the Hungarian–Austrian border on August 21, 1989. But since 1979, Hungarian citizens could visit Austria without visas, while East Germans suffered extralegal persecution just for filing a formal request to travel or even emigrate to the non-socialist world.[7] At other stretches of the external borders of the Socialist Camp, however, the Iron Curtain was not even fortified, with people and animals crossing back and forth.

Traditionally, borders have served multiple purposes. Delineated border lines mark where one state ends and another one begins. Fortifications primarily functioned as a military deterrence between hostile neighbors. Secured borders and designated entry/exit points operated to control people from crossing in either direction. Customarily, modern states were interested in controlling who was entering, that is, in filtering desirable from undesirable visitors. Yet, the

---

[5] *WP*, 12/6/1961:A1; *CDT*, 11/15/1961:5; *Sun*, 4/10/1978:A2; *Newsday*, 9/17/1979:1Q; Dietmar Arnold, and Sven Felix Kellerhoff, *Unterirdisch in die Freiheit* (Ch. Links, 2015); *HC*, 3/7/1967:1a; Sven Felix Kellerhoff, Lars-Broder Keil, and Thomas Schmid, *Mord an der Mauer* (Quadriga, 2012).

[6] Gerhard Sälter, Johanna Dietrich, and Fabian Kuhn, *Die vergessenen Toten* (Ch. Links, 2016), pp. 97–238; Hans-Hermann Hertle, *Die Todesopfer an der Berliner Mauer 1961–1989* (Bundeszentrale für politische Bildung, 2020), p. 22; Klaus Schroeder and Jochen Staadt, *Die Todesopfer des DDR-Grenzregimes an der innerdeutschen Grenze 1949–1989* (Bundeszentrale für politische Bildung, 2007). The statistics do not include death by drowning in the Baltic Sea or the killing of GDR citizens trying to cross other borders.

[7] Dieter Szorger and Pia Bayer, *Das Burgenland und der Fall des Eisernen Vorhangs* (Amt der Burgenländischen Landesregierung. 2009), pp. 13–16; Hans-Hermann Lochen, "Die geheimgehaltenen Bestimmungen über das Ausreiseverfahren als Ausdruck staatlicher Willkür,"; Bernd Eisenfeld, Hans H. Lochen, Irena Kukutz, Werner Hilse, and Joachim Gauck, *Ausreisen oder dableiben?* 2nd ed (BStU, 1998), pp. 20–29.

external borders of the former socialist states, particularly their borders to non-socialist states, were almost *unique* in recent history, as we will see in the following nine sections. Their fortifications were *primarily* designed to keep people from leaving in the first place. In many respects, these barriers were the last of a series of obstacles – legal and physical – for anybody attempting to depart. Citizens who tried to exit legally needed to get a passport and an exit visa (i.e., the permission to leave legally), both of which often were nearly impossible to obtain. The fortification of borders and the danger of being killed by trying to cross them illegally served for many as a deterrent not to try at all. A nonagenarian family friend, who had lived her whole life in East Berlin, once told this author that she would not have gone even near the East German borders, because everybody knew that "they" – the border guards – would shoot to kill. In the Soviet Union of the 1930s, the existence of both fortified borders and the repressive state equally served as psychological deterrence not to request a passport or an exit visa.[8]

Hence, leaving illegally often was the only path for the courageous few, but it required planning, preparations, and subterfuge. This included scouting out suitable border areas, surreptitiously hand-copying border area maps in public libraries, as well as preparing food, clothes, vehicles, and other necessary items. However, escapes often did not go beyond the planning stage since security services were vigilant. Between 1961 and 1989, around 75,000 GDR citizens were arrested while preparing to escape or during the attempt itself, according to the best estimates. If not discovered early on, illegal border crossers still had to surmount a set of obstacles, including restricted border areas several kilometers wide, minefields, barbed wires, electrical fences, trip wires that released signal flares and alarmed fast-shooting border guards, and, in the case of East Germany, automatic self-shooting mechanisms and the actual wall.[9]

Given the prominence of the term *Iron Curtain* in Western rhetoric during the Cold War and in the later historiography, the actual borders of the Socialist Camp have attracted surprisingly little scholarly attention, except for the massive number of specialized publications on the borders dividing Berlin and Germany. Cold War historians have used the Iron Curtain mainly as a metaphor for the East–West division, as a synonym for the Soviet oppression of East European peoples after 1945, or as a marker of the start of the global

---

[8] Andrea Chandler, *Institutions of Isolation* (McGill-Queen's University Press, 1998), pp. 18–23, 74–77.

[9] *LAT*, 12/26/1980:C7; *WP*, 11/15/1961:A1; Gerhard Sälter, *Das Grenzregime im Zentrum Berlins* (Ch. Links, 2018), p. 43; Gordon L. Rottman and Chris Taylor, *The Berlin Wall and the Inner-German Border 1961–89* (Osprey, 2008).

conflict.[10] Authors interested in the actual border lines and areas have mainly focused on its ecological meaning for declining plant and animal species during the Cold War, or on how it has come to look afterwards.[11]

The external borders of the Socialist Camp consisted of several sectors, interrupted by large bodies of water like the Baltic Sea, the Black Sea, the Caspian Sea, the South China Sea, the Yellow Sea, the Sea of Japan, the North Pacific Ocean, and the Bering Sea. The principal stretch on land was the Central European sector that divided the continent along the western borders of East Germany, Czechoslovakia, Hungary, and Yugoslavia. After the 1950s, though, Cold War observers no longer considered Yugoslavia to belong to the Socialist Camp and hence inside the Iron Curtain.[12] Unlike the other external borders of the Socialist Camp, the Central European sector of the Iron Curtain cut through densely populated territories that had long historical, economic, political, and personal connections with each other – most importantly in the form of pre-1945 Germany, the pre-1918 Austro-Hungarian Empire, and historically mixed ethnic settlement patterns. Millions of people still passed across the Central European sector in the immediate post–World War II period. Only by the late 1940s did the emerging communist regimes in Yugoslavia, Hungary, and Czechoslovakia – but not East Germany – begin to fortify their borders for a variety of reasons: to prevent political dissidents from leaving in order to organize political activities abroad, to arrest them for punishment, or to retain their own people for mainly economic reasons. It was this particular sector that Churchill had in mind when he gave his Iron Curtain speech in March of 1946.

Yet, Western Cold War rhetoric soon applied the term Iron Curtain to all sectors of the external borders of the Socialist Camp. The Nordic sector, running through forests and waterways, separated the USSR from Finland and Norway. The Balkan sector split Albania, Yugoslavia, and Bulgaria from Greece and Turkey. The mountainous Caucasian sector separated the Soviet Union from Turkey and Iran. The Iron Curtain then followed through deserts, in the fairways of rivers, and along the Himalayas to Southeast Asia. Finally, its East Asian

---

[10] Patrick Wright, *Iron Curtain* (Oxford University Press, 2007); Anne Applebaum, *Iron Curtain* (Anchor Books, 2013); Mark Kramer and Vit Smetana, eds., *Imposing, Maintaining, and Tearing Open the Iron Curtain* (Lexington Books, 2014); Vernon Bartlett, *East of the Iron Curtain* (Latimer House, 1949); John Gunther, *Behind the Curtain* (Harper, 1949); Poul Villaume and O. Arne Westad, eds., *Perforating the Iron Curtain* (Museum Tusculanum Press, 2010); Fraser J. Harbutt, *The Iron Curtain* (Oxford University Press, 1986); Pierre de Senarclens, *From Yalta to the Iron Curtain* (Berg, 1995).

[11] Astrid M. Eckert, *West Germany and the Iron Curtain* (Oxford University Press, 2019); Timothy Phillips, *Retracing the Iron Curtain* (The Experiment, 2022); Peter Laufer, *Iron Curtain Rising* (Mercury House, 1991); Sonja K. Pieck, *Mnemonic Ecologies* (MIT Press, 2023).

[12] *JP*, 7/15/1953:4.

variation detached Hong Kong and Macao from communist mainland China after 1949 and has partitioned Korea since 1953.

Moreover, Western rhetoric did not always match the reality and location of the fortified and closed socialist borders that emerged in the Cold War. The external borders of the Socialist Camp ranged widely from hardly demarcated boundary lines to border strips sporting walls. Yet almost the same kind of borders *also* appeared at some of the boundaries *between socialist states* in East Europe, revealing ethnic and political fault lines similar to those between the Cold War blocs. In the early 1950s, for example, Romania's border to Hungary looked remarkably similar to Hungary's border to Austria. But these kinds of fortified boundaries, including depopulated border zones, appeared almost *exclusively* at the borders of socialist states – and virtually nowhere else – during the Cold War.

On the whole, the post–World War II Iron Curtain emerged in the historical context of international, Imperial Russian, and Soviet interwar border controls. Before World War I, the movement of people within Europe, the Northern Atlantic world, and the Americas had been surprisingly unconstrained, although numerous restrictions applied to the rest of the world and particularly to colonial subjects. Both global wars witnessed the introduction of entry visas for non-citizens and exit visas for both citizens and non-citizens. Only few states – among them the United States, the United Kingdom, and France – completely lifted these rigid wartime restrictions after the end of either hostility.[13] Yet, in the context of the evolving Cold War, the US Department of State denied passports to individual American citizens who were suspected of pro-Soviet sympathies, although the Supreme Court eventually terminated this practice in 1958. Still, in 1921 and 1926, the League of Nations hosted two conferences to reestablish visa-free travel at a global level, but with little success. Similarly, the United Nations discussed the problem in 1947, largely under pressure from American tourist organizations and Western chambers of commerce concerned about the continued negative impact of closed borders to the free movement of people and goods.[14]

1 Soviet Interwar Borders

A relatively small, but excellent, body of historiography helps us to outline the development of Soviet citizenship laws, passport regulations, exit visa practices, and border controls during the interwar period. These two decades

---

[13] John Torpey, *The Invention of the Passport* (Cambridge University Press, 2000), pp. 93–116; *NYTribune*, 7/26/1919:3; *Sun*, 8/30/1945:12; *Tat*, 9/26/1945:7; *Bund*-m, 3/7/1946:2.

[14] *CDT*, 4/3/1948:A4; *NYT*, 8/24/1948:10; *GM*, 8/4/1950:2; *NYT*, 6/17/1958:1; *Observer*, 4/24/1921:7; *NYT*, 1/22/1946:4; *NYT*, 1/8/1947:4; *NYT*, 3/15/1947:3; *CSM*, 4/14/1947:7.

witnessed a change from relative openness in the 1920s to almost complete and fortified self-isolation in the 1930s. After the October Revolution in late 1917, a significant number of mostly urbanites and then White Russians fled the country out of fear of persecution. The new government lacked the means to stop this exodus, despite the introduction of passport and exit/entry rules in late 1917. By mid-1921, Soviet authorities decided to denaturalize 1.5 million Russian refugees that refused to apply for a Soviet passport from abroad. The relatively few returnees that had accepted Soviet citizenship underwent mandatory police registration on arrival and then were prohibited from leaving Soviet Russia/the USSR ever again.[15]

Nevertheless, legal exit remained possible until the late 1920s. The vast majority of the more than 600,000 people leaving legally in that decade were prisoners of war and individuals who opted for non-Soviet citizenship. From the establishment of the USSR in 1922 to approximately 1928 most Soviet citizens were still allowed to travel abroad with a valid passport and an exit visa, provided they had entry visas to other countries. However, by 1926, the passport fees had become prohibitive – 200 rubles (amounting to circa three monthly wages; equaling 100 US$) for workers, and 300 (150 US$) for all others. During the 1921–26 period, for which data is available, almost 200,000 Soviet citizens lawfully exited on external travel. Starting in 1924, Soviet citizens who had left legally but refused to return also were deprived of their citizenship. Authorities increasingly worried about the continued exit of limited hard currency available, which led to a further restriction of access to valuta and hence the opportunity to travel abroad.[16]

At the end of the Civil War in 1922, illegal border crossings in either direction formally became criminal offenses, while stricter border controls were introduced. The Criminal Code of 1922/24 punished offenders with "compulsory labour or imprisonment for a period of up to six months, or with a fine up to 500 roubles." In 1934, exiting the Soviet Union without permission even could lead to charges of treason. Two years later, the fine was dropped but the penalty increased to "confinement in a [corrective labor] camp for a period of from one to 3 years." Both the application of these rules and the progressively well-guarded Soviet borders to the Baltic states, Poland, and Romania had a negative

---

[15] Eric Lohr, *Soviet Citizenship* (Harvard University Press, 2012), p. 145; Chandler, *Institutions of Isolation*, pp. 34, 147–48; Yuri Felshtinsky, "The Legal Foundations of the Immigration and Emigration Policy of the USSR," *Soviet Studies*, 34/3 (1982), p. 328.

[16] Valerian V. Obolensky-Ossinsky, "Emigration from and Immigration into Russia," Walter F. Willcox, ed., *International Migrations*, vol. II (National Bureau of Economic Research, 1931), pp. 571–72; Albert Baiburin, *The Soviet Passport* (Polity, 2021), pp. 23, 54–55; Felshtinsky, "The Legal Foundations," pp. 340–42; Chandler, *Institutions of Isolation*, pp. 52, 71, 74; *CSM*, 8/10/1922:11; *NYT*, 4/8/1926:27.

impact on historical cross-border relations. Given the hostile relations to its Central European neighbors and the operations of anti-Bolshevik organizations, the USSR refused to enter into agreements allowing cross-border contacts between local populations there, in contrast to its practice at its Caucasian border with Turkey and Persia/Iran.[17]

As early as May 1918, the Bolshevik regime decreed the creation of designated border zones where buildings and agricultural cultivation were slated for removal. In 1922, Soviet authorities reestablished a border guard corps similar to the Tsarist predecessor after the boundaries of the first communist state with neighboring European states had been stabilized following years of military conflict. The recreated border guard corps was put under the supervision of the secret police – the Cheka and later the *GPU* (State Political Directorate, renamed in 1923 to *OGPU*/Joint State Political Directorate). In 1923, Soviet authorities also created a layered border regime of a 4-meter-wide border strip, a 500-meter-wide border zone, a 7.5-kilometer-wide border area, and a 22-kilometer-wide border region.[18]

The subsequent development of the Soviet border guard corps occurred in unison with similar developments in the Baltic states, Poland, and Romania. Its task was both defensive in terms of border protection against neighboring states and émigré agitation and offensive in terms of disinformation warfare and political infiltration. In January 1925, the Politburo of the Communist Party of the Soviet Union (CPSU) set the number of border guards at 31,500 men, of whom 30 percent served at the Central European border sector.[19]

In the early 1920s, Soviet authorities formally reintroduced Tsarist regulations on the use of physical force at its borders. In February 1921, the regulations of 1912 authorizing the use of weapons to stop anybody escaping pursuit, regardless of direction, were reinstated. They primarily focused on suppressing smuggling into and out of Soviet Russia/USSR. In 1923, the Imperial Russian prohibition to shoot across the border into the neighboring country was formally reintroduced and kept in place until 1960, although it was not always observed, as we will see later. In March that year, Soviet authorities also defined for the

---

[17] Russia [R.S.F.S.R.], *The Criminal Code of the Russian Socialist Federative Soviet Republic [1922–24]* (His Majesty's Stationary Office, 1925), p. 25 (first quote); Sabine Dullin, *La frontière épaisse* (EHESS, 2014), pp. 242–44; second quote in: United States, Central Intelligence Agency, Foreign Documents Division, *RSFSR Criminal Code, 1956 edition* (CIA, 1958), p. 43 (brackets in original); Dullin, *La frontière épaisse*, pp. 116–118, 150–51; Chandler, *Institutions of Isolation*, p. 32.

[18] Chandler, *Institutions of Isolation*, p. 38; Dullin, *La frontière épaisse*, pp. 42–43, 83, 103–7; Terry Martin, *The Affirmative Action State* (Cornell University Press, 2001), p. 314.

[19] Dullin, *La frontière épaisse*, pp. 46–56, 154–55, 162–68.

first time an even more extensive high-security region along the entire sea and land border, where the GPU/OGPU had unlimited rights of search and seizure.[20]

In 1928, the USSR ended almost all external travel and legal emigration, although trusted citizens on official missions were still allowed to leave for certain periods of time. Some nevertheless defected while abroad. But for private citizens, it was nearly impossible to obtain passports and exit visas – mainly for five interrelated reasons. First, the emerging Stalinist state sought self-isolation from the outside world. Since the late 1920s, it had grown concerned with the possibility that Soviet citizens, even on official missions, returned with subversive ideas. Second, the USSR by 1928 had managed to conclude border and citizenship agreements with neighboring countries that removed uncertainties and loopholes which individuals could exploit to exit the country.[21]

Third, the Soviet government needed to retain labor at any cost for its modernization and industrialization projects. Preventing illegal border crossings, even with brutal force as we will see later, served as a tool of population control and a deterrent for copycats. In 1932, the USSR also introduced internal passports to control domestic population movements. Not every Soviet citizen received such a passport; those without were prohibited from settling in cities, industrial areas, and sensitive border zones. Similar to the introduction of the rigid emigration/immigration policies since 1928, the internal passport was a "social filter" between reliable/desirable and unreliable/undesirable persons.[22]

Fourth, the Soviet state wanted to preserve and even increase its foreign currency holdings. Hence, it focused on spending valuta on importing machinery for industrialization instead of providing citizens with the means for foreign travel. In that vein, it even decided in 1930 to stop all of the remaining emigration to the United States in order to benefit from the continued remittances from relatives living there. In late 1932, the cost for an exit visa was sharply increased to 500 rubles (250 US$) for workers and 1,000 rubles (500 US$) for everybody else, to be paid in foreign currency.[23]

---

[20] Andrey Shlyakhter, "Smuggler states," dissertation, University of Chicago, 2020. My thanks to Andrey for the reference to the two Imperial regulations, see in: I. A. Doroshenko eds., *Iz istorii voisk VChK i pogranichnoi okhrany* (Voenisdat, 1958), pp. 435–36, and I. A. Doroshenko, eds., *Iz istorii sovetskikh pogranichnych voisk, 1921–1927* (Voenisdat, 1963), pp. 294–95; Dullin, *La frontière épaisse*, p. 128; Martin, *Affirmative Action State*, p. 314; Chandler, *Institutions of Isolation*, pp. 35–37, 40, 49–51, 63.

[21] Chandler, *Institutions of Isolation*, pp. 73–78; Erik R. Scott, *Defectors* (Oxford University Press, 2023), pp. 14–15; Lohr, *Soviet Citizenship*, pp. 170, 175; Felshtinsky, "The Legal Foundations," p. 342.

[22] Baiburin, *Soviet Passport*, pp. 58–63.

[23] Lohr, *Soviet Citizenship*, p. 173; *CDT*, 10/21/1930:17; *CDH*, 11/30/1932:1; *NYT*, 12/1/1932:1; *JA*, 9/4/1936:10; Baiburin, *Soviet Passport*, p. 55.

Finally, the grain crisis in 1928 and the Soviet decision to introduce agricultural collectivization late the following year inaugurated a radical tightening of the border regime. Within a year, illegal entries from the Soviet Union to Poland quintupled to over 2,500, according to official Polish statistics. But a Polish report also mentioned that "many residents of the border villages managed to escape to Poland" in early 1930 while Soviet border guards were engaging in "'hunts' for kulaks who are trying to sneak across the border."[24] In December of 1929 alone, Polish border guards reportedly apprehended 850 illegal entries from the USSR, of which 100 were expellees and 34 Soviet secret couriers. Within three months, the Polish government announced its intentions to keep its borders open for refugees from Soviet collectivization, particularly for those with Polish ancestry, and to set up camps to house them temporarily.[25] By March of 1930, the repression of Soviet citizens of Polish origin in Ukraine started with mass deportations to the Soviet interior, leading to a further increase of escapes to Poland.[26] From 1931 to 1933, OGPU border units also machine-gunned refugees attempting to flee en masse to Romania, including the firing across the border line. Hundreds died trying to cross the Dniester River into Romania – on boats or by swimming in the summer and on horse-drawn sleds in the winter, and thousands were arrested in the attempt to flee. Yet, thousands probably still managed to escape.[27]

At the turn of 1929/30, Soviet authorities started to remove minority populations – particularly Poles and Germans – into the Soviet interior. As local authorities put it, the policy served to cleanse border districts from "pollution."[28] At the same time, the USSR began to plan the fortification of the entire western land border. In August of 1932, the OGPU reportedly cleared a 20-kilometer-wide area on the Soviet side of the border by removing residents and destroying all unnecessary buildings. In May 1933, the area was extended to a region of 60 kilometers at some border stretches, which would explain the drop of escapes reported in the Western newspapers.[29]

In 1932, American media offered a vivid description of the actual Soviet border stretching from the Arctic to the Black Sea. Encompassing only twelve entry/exit points, this combined Nordic and Central European border line was

---

[24] Republic of Poland, *Korpus Ochrony Pogranicza*, vols. *1928–1929* and *1929–1930* (Wydawnictwo oficerów i szeregowych korpusu ochr. Pogranicza, [1930? & 1931?]), pp. 15 and 10, 54–57 (quote), respectively.
[25] *BT*, 12/18/1929:3; *Sun*, 3/2/1930:10; *NYT*, 3/7/1930:6.
[26] Martin, *Affirmative Action State*, pp. 321–22.
[27] Eduard Baidaus, "The River that Killed and Saved," *Journal of Romanian Studies*, 6/1 (2024), pp. 15–23; *NYT*, 3/6/1931:15; *SCMP*, 1/20/1932:10; *NYT*, 2/25/1932:2; *SCMP*, 3/1/1933:12.
[28] Dullin, *La frontière épaisse*, pp. 168–69, 175, 214 (quote).
[29] *Bund*-e, 8/11/1932:2; *Bund*-m, 12/20/1937:6; *Newsweek*, 5/6/1933:15.

heavily guarded but hardly fortified. The border ran through circa 1,500 kilometers of pine forests in the Nordic sector and through around 3,000 kilometers of arable plains and mountain ranges along the Baltic states, Poland, and Romania. Even if the Soviet–Finnish border was difficult-to-patrol terrain, the sparsely populated and generally wild regions on both sides made escapes rare. At the Baltic-Polish-Romanian border line, however, Soviet guards patrolled on horses, sometimes accompanied by similar units from the neighboring state riding in parallel on the other side. Fraternization between corresponding units was neither possible nor desired; the few formal contacts remained stiff and short. But in between patrols, people continued to cross the border line.[30]

The systematic fortification of the entire western border line started as late as 1935. Initially, this comprised the completion of a continuous forbidden-access zone on the Soviet side, followed by the establishment of physical barriers near the boundary line itself. Between 1935 and 1938, the Soviet government removed around 100,000 Poles, Finns, Karelians, Ingrians, Balts, Kurds, Armenians, and Turks from the entire western and Caucasian border regions to the Soviet interior in order to strengthen security by cutting all connections to neighboring countries (Map 2). Paradoxically, Stalin's agreement with Nazi Germany's Adolf Hitler to divide Poland in late August of 1939 and the subsequent Soviet land grabs along the entire Baltic-Polish-Romanian border required the replication of border securitization and population removal in territories hundreds of kilometers further west until the German attack in June of 1941.[31]

Soviet peasants fled not only across the western borders in the 1930s but also across their Siberian and Central Asian counterparts. In the spring of 1930, hundreds of peasants from virtually the whole Soviet Union arrived on a daily basis in Harbin, the Russian-built but Chinese, later Japanese imperial, railroad town in northern Manchuria. Without job prospects in Harbin's depressed urban economy, Soviet peasant refugees were entirely dependent on the charity of the small White Russian émigré population.[32] By the spring of 1930 as well, Kazakh nomads tried to flee collectivization to Xinjiang. Although many succeeded, thousands were killed by Soviet border guards in 1930 and 1931. Much of the violence occurred in the context of ongoing territorial disputes and Soviet attempts since the late 1920s to suppress organized smuggling activities. Yet, at the Tajik border to Afghanistan, where Soviet authorities almost

---

[30] *Enquirer Sunday Magazine*, 4/24/1932:3; *NYT*, 8/14/1930:9.
[31] Dullin, *La frontière épaisse*, pp. 227–30, 237; Alexander Statiev, "Soviet Ethnic Deportations," *Journal of Genocide Research*, 11 (2009), pp. 243–44; Oksana Ermolaeva, "Border Control and Early Soviet Statehood," *Ab Imperio*, 4 (2022), p. 119; Martin, *Affirmative Action State*, pp. 328–29; Martin, "Origins," pp. 846–52.
[32] *CP*, 4/7/1930:1; *CP*, 4/23/1930:6; *CWR*, 7/5/1930:180; *CDT*, 1/11/1931:F8; *CP*, 3/6/1931:8; *Enquirer Sunday Magazine*, 4/24/1932:3.

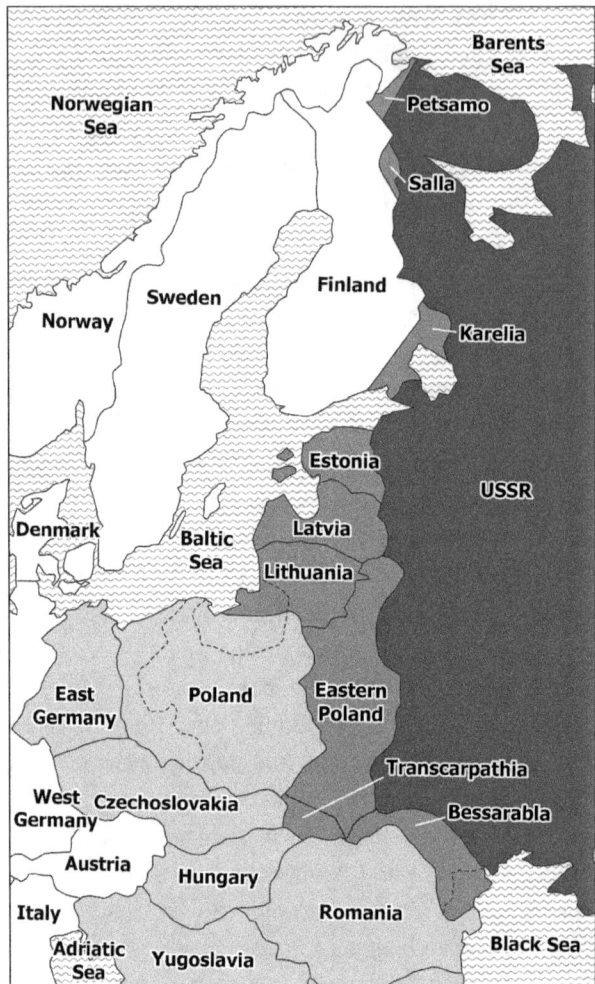

Map 2 Soviet interwar borders

completely lacked human resources, the USSR succeeded over the course of the 1920s and 1930s to bind local populations with cross-border contacts into the unitary Soviet state by employing a mix of harsh resettlement strategies and conciliatory policies.

2 *Churchill's Iron Curtain* in East Europe

The scholarly literature and available source material on borders between the USSR and East Europe as well as within that semi-continent are surprisingly limited, which permits only a sketch in broad strokes. The citizenship laws, exit regulations, and border fortifications that the emerging communist regimes in

Soviet-occupied East Europe adopted in and after 1947 looked eerily similar to Soviet interwar and concurrent practices. None of the East European communist regimes, however, adopted the Soviet border model completely, but usually integrated parts into preexisting practices that had emerged independently since 1945.[33] Astonishingly, the Iron Curtain dividing Europe into a communist East and a non-communist West was not unique. Similarly fortified borders also emerged *between* communist states early on, largely to prevent illegal border crossing (usually from East to West) or to cut ties to neighboring states.

World War II had brought unimaginable destruction and loss of life to the USSR. The task of reconstructing the partially destroyed country required enormous amounts of labor and investment. Given the interwar attitude of the Soviet government toward the control of its citizens, the Stalinist regime insisted on the mandatory return of all Soviet citizens – former prisoners of war, forced laborers, and displaced persons – to the USSR. As one historian suggested, the Soviet regime considered its citizens as akin to state property.[34]

In this context, the interwar prohibition to emigrate remained on the books into the post–World War II period. Yet, the war had moved frontiers further west because the USSR had occupied the Baltic states and annexed Eastern Poland, Slovak Transcarpathia, and Romanian Bessarabia (today's Moldova) (Map 2). Ethnic Germans (*Volksdeutsche*), Jews, Poles, Slovaks, and Romanians from newly Soviet-occupied territories moved west, sometimes with Soviet approval and encouragement, while Soviet citizens – former forced laborers and prisoners of war – went the other way. Yet, legal emigration from the USSR, including renunciation of Soviet citizenship, remained only possible by explicit approval of the central government.[35] In order to deter other avenues of emigration, the late Stalinist regime prohibited marriage between Soviet citizens and foreigners in 1947. It hence did not even allow hundreds of Soviet spouses of Western diplomatic personnel, journalists, and other citizens to leave together with their partners. The diplomatic tug-of-war to lift this prohibition lasted until after Stalin's death in March of 1953.[36]

The strict border regimes of the 1930s also applied to the new Soviet postwar borders, even if our knowledge of the actual nature of the fortified border line to Central Europe from 1945 to 1989 remains scant.[37] In the year of Stalin's death, 223,000 border guards protected Soviet borders, to be reduced by 90,000 over

---

[33] As suggested for the security services by: Molly Pucci, *Security Empire* (Yale University, 2020).
[34] Sheila Fitzpatrick, *Lost Souls* (Princeton University Press, 2024).
[35] Chandler, *Institutions of Isolation*, pp. 81–82; Mark Wyman, *DPs* (Cornell University Press, 2015), pp. 17–22, 64; Sarah Cameron, *The Hungry Steppe* (Cornell University Press, 2019), p. 123; Robert Kindler, *Stalin's Nomads* (University of Pittsburgh Press, 2018), pp. 141–45; George Ginsburgs, *The Citizenship Law of the USSR* (Springer, 1983), p. 230.
[36] *LAT*, 4/6/1947:6; *NYT*, 6/10/1953:1. [37] Amy Knight, *The KGB* (Routledge, 2021), p. 232.

the next two years as de-Stalinization started.[38] By 1983, it had reached around 200,000 again, and six years later, even slightly more.[39]

Documents of the American Central Intelligence Agency (CIA) provide us with one of the few overviews of the nature of the Soviet borders to Poland, Czechoslovakia, Hungary, and Romania in the early 1950s. Only after signing border treaties and completing demarcation with all four states by the late 1940s did the USSR start to secure its new borders. Apart from a few entry/exit points, the fortifications were primarily designed to prevent Soviet citizens, who could not emigrate legally, from doing so illegally. The actual border consisted of a 10- to 15-meter-wide plowed strip that was cleared of vegetation and contained stacked barbed wire rolls, electrical fences, watchtowers, searchlights, trip wires with signal flares, and armed border patrols on both sides. Yet, the Soviet side of the border generally was controlled more strictly, with a 15- to 32-kilometer-wide border area, where trusted populations lived under tight control, and another adjacent region that could reach a further 80 kilometers into the Soviet interior. By 1949, ethnic Poles who had not opted to emigrate to Poland were deported to the Soviet interior.[40]

The post-Stalin leadership decided in 1953 to dismantle parts of the border fortifications and abolish travel prohibitions to neighboring socialist states. The significant geographical extent of the layered border zone had left large parts of the peripheral USSR underdeveloped. Hence, the actual restricted border zone shrank to a strip only of 20 meters for patrol paths and border markers. In 1955, Soviet authorities also allowed business, tourist, and personal trips to the socialist countries of East Europe, followed by permissions for similar trips to the non-socialist world in the early 1960s.[41]

The emigration of Soviet Jews, who had campaigned for the right to leave since Stalin's death, started in the late 1960s, particularly after the Six-Day War in June 1967. By 1971, the Soviet government formally allowed all Soviet citizens to emigrate; yet, during the 1970s, the vast majority of the 300,000 emigrants were Jews, followed by smaller numbers of Germans and Armenians.[42] In the 1970s, the USSR however seemed to return to some of the strict border regulations of the 1930s and the post–World War II period; a Western newspaper reported in 1981

---

[38] Sabine Dullin, "Des frontières s'ouvrent et se ferment," *Relations Internationales*, 3/147 (2011), p. 41.
[39] V. I. Boyarsky, *Na strazhe granits otechestva* (Moskva, 1998), p. 514.
[40] FOIA Reading Room: CIA-RDP08C01297R000500010011-6, p. 76–81, 87–89, 101–3; CIA-RDP82-00457R003800590003-7; also: *GM*, 9/13/1949:7.
[41] Dullin, "Des frontières s'ouvrent et se ferment," pp. 41–48; Diane P. Koenker, *Club Red* (Cornell University Press, 216), pp. 210–11.
[42] Gennady Estraikh, *Jews in the Soviet Union*, vol. 5, *After Stalin, 1953–1967* (New York University Press, 2022); Zvi Gitelman, "Exiting from the Soviet Union," *Michigan Journal of International Law*, 3/1 (1982), pp. 43–44.

about the reappearance of minefields, for example. In October 1989, eventually, the KGB announced its intention to simplify border crossing rules, to take down fortifications, and to reduce the 3.6 million square kilometers of restricted border regions – equaling on average a 60-kilometer-wide belt along the entire land and sea border – by 90 percent.[43]

*

The borders within Soviet-occupied East Europe displayed a wide variety of characteristics, from close similarities to the Soviet western border in the late Stalinist period to relative openness. Although comparatively little evidence is available, CIA records provide us with an impression from the early 1950s. The legacies of the Habsburg Empire and opposing alliance choices during World War II had left many East European states in 1945 with distrust of their own ethnic minorities. Romania and Czechoslovakia, for example, considered their Hungarian minorities a security threat. After 1948, the Hungarian–Romanian border looked like a double Iron Curtain, consisting of parallel lines of watchtowers, minefields, and barbed wire entanglements. Romania even established a 5-kilometer-wide area from where local populations had been removed and 30-kilometer-wide region with restricted access.[44]

But other borders between the emerging socialist states in East Europe were less fortified. In the 1950s, the Polish–Czechoslovak border sported only border markers. The relatively short East German–Polish land border west of Szczecin/Stettin was only lightly fortified with watchtowers and trip wires connected to signal flares. The plowed strip on the Polish side suggests that the installations primarily served to prevent illegal exit from East to West. Corresponding units from each country collaborated in managing the joint border. Similarly, river borders within East Europe generally were only lightly guarded. The Romanian–Bulgarian border along the Danube remained unfortified on either side, largely because illegal border crossings virtually did not occur. Communist party members from either side could cross the few bridges simply by showing their party membership card as an ID; ordinary citizens needed a passport and an entry visa. Yet, the East German–Polish Oder–Neisse line sported patrol boats, watchtowers on both riverbanks, and a small number of tightly controlled bridges.[45]

Immediately after the end of World War II, Soviet military units guarded the western borders of Hungary (to Austria) and Czechoslovakia (to Austria and Germany). Units of the NKVD (People's Commissariat for Internal Affairs)

---

[43] Chandler, *Institutions of Isolation*, pp. 84, 88; *JE*, 2/6/1981:5; *GM*, 10/21/1989:A4.
[44] FOIA Reading Room: CIA-RDP80-00809A000700120280-6.
[45] FOIA Reading Room: CIA-RDP82-00047R000400010009-6, CIA-RDP80T00246A04800050 0001-3, CIA-RDP82-00457R011300060005-9.

staffed the western control lines of the Soviet zones of occupation in Austria and in Germany, both of which bordered the British and American counterparts in either country. Still, all of these state borders and control lines remained relatively open in the early postwar period, largely because the USSR and Soviet-occupied East European countries formally expelled or simply drove out over 12 million ethnic Germans and around a quarter of a million Jews.[46]

The expulsion of ethnic Germans from East Europe started in late 1944, creating large treks of people moving from Eastern Europe to the Allied zones of occupation in Germany and Austria. Only in the fall of 1945 did the four Allies and several governments of the Soviet-occupied East European countries agree on an orderly and methodical population transfer. Particularly the Western Allies were concerned about the sudden and unorganized arrival of millions of refugees in semi-destroyed and starving Germany and Austria. Most *Volksdeutsche* from the Baltic states and Poland fled to the Soviet zone of occupation in Germany. Most other ethnic Germans fled to Vienna, from where they were transported to the Western occupation zones of Germany. The *Sudetendeutsche* in western Czechoslovakia were expelled to the American and Soviet zones of occupation in Germany.[47]

The flight of Jewish populations started with the delay of approximately half a year. Widespread anti-Semitism and conflict over property restitution, rather than government policies, caused the desire of many Jews to leave. A few of the Polish Jews chose to flee to Berlin, while the vast majority of East European Jews escaped to Vienna, from where they either traveled to Italy for illegal passage to Palestine or were transferred to Germany into American-run camps for displaced persons. While the Polish state tried to sell exit visas to Jews, the Allies themselves hoped to prevent the arrival of Jews in Berlin and Vienna. The four occupation powers were already overwhelmed by the influx of ethnic German expellees into the German capital and the surrounding Soviet zone of occupation. In early 1946, they agreed to close the new German–Polish border to Jewish refugees, who nevertheless managed to cross in the thousands. Late that fall, Poland closed its border to Czechoslovakia for Jewish emigrants bound for Vienna, as did Soviet occupation forces in Austria. The double closing did not happen for the purpose of keeping Jews in Eastern Europe, but on request from the UK government to prevent them from illegally emigrating to Palestine. In 1946, the lowering of

---

[46] Rottman/Taylor, *Berlin Wall*, p. 42; Eagle Glassheim, "National Mythologies and Ethnic Cleansing," *Central European History*, 33/4 (2000), p. 465; Jeffrey Veidlinger, "One Doesn't Make out Much with Furs in Palestine," *East European Jewish Affairs*, 44/2–3 (2014), p. 241.

[47] Raymond M. Douglas, *Orderly and Humane* (Yale University Press, 2012).

Churchill's Iron Curtain stretching from the Baltic to the Adriatic was partially the result of British policy, though not his own.[48]

As we will see, Churchill's Iron Curtain eventually started to descend at Hungary's western border in late 1947, one and a half years after his famous Fulton speech. The closure of Czechoslovakia's western border followed in the spring of 1948, but the East German border to West Germany was fortified only after May 1952. Subsequently, only the East German and East Berlin borders to West Berlin remained open for another nine years and three months. Yet, there were two exceptional periods in this overall trend between 1947 and 1961. During the Berlin blockade from June 1948 to May 1949, the USSR closed access to West Berlin for goods (but not for people), with the Anglo-American occupation powers reacting with the sealing of the West German border to East Germany in an economic counterblockade. And in the wake of the June Uprising in East Germany in 1953, Soviet occupation troops and the East German regime closed land access to West Berlin for people during a short period of time.[49] But there was one exemption to all these developments – Yugoslavia.

3 Yugoslavia's Iron Curtains, 1945–1965

"Little attempt has been made to erect an 'iron curtain' along the Yugoslav border," a CIA report stated in 1960, although not completely correctly.[50] At the most southern stretch of Churchill's Iron Curtain, the evolving East–West conflict became entangled with preexisting territorial disputes and then the Soviet–Yugoslav Split. In the spring of 1948, the Balkan country started to fortify its borders to Austria in order to prevent illegal exit. A year later, a firm Iron Curtain had descended on Yugoslavia's border with its socialist neighbors Hungary, Romania, and Bulgaria while its border to Albania tightened. The Soviet–Yugoslav Split, however, helped to end Yugoslav support for the communist rebels in the Greek Civil War, as described in Section 9.

Yugoslavia's communist government assumed power at the end of World War II without Soviet aid and occupation troops. Its rise triggered several waves of refugees to Austria and Italy for various causes – government-sponsored ethnic cleansing, political persecution, unwillingness to serve in the Yugoslav army, or catastrophic economic developments.[51] By mid-1946, more than 10,000 Yugoslavs and more than 60,000 ethnic Germans had arrived in Austria. A

---

[48] Jan T. Gross, *Fear* (Random House, 2006); Thomas Albrich and Ronald W. Zweig, eds., *Escape through Austria* (Frank Cass, 2002); *NYT*, 10/7/1945:15; *PP*, 9/25/1945:3; *JA*, 1/3/1946:3; *BT*, 9/26/1946:3; *NZZ*-e, 9/30/1946:2.
[49] Ilko-Sascha Kowalczuk, *17. Juni 1953* (Bundeszentrale für politische Bildung, 2013), p. 51.
[50] FOIA Reading Room: CIA-RDP80T00246A053500130001-3, p. 7.
[51] *Tat*, 5/15/1947:2; *NZZ*-e, 3/18/1948:2; *CSM*, 4/10/1948:13; *NZZ*-e, 6/4/1948:2.

year later, five hundred to one thousand Yugoslav citizens and four thousand to five thousand ethnic Germans fled to Austria every month – often without any papers. Soon thereafter, Yugoslavia tried to prevent further escapes by declaring a 5-kilometer-wide area at the borders to Austria and Italy off limits to civilians; offenders could be shot and killed without warning. Half a year later, the area was extended to 15 kilometers.[52]

Like Stalin, Yugoslavia's Josip Broz Tito aspired to territorial aggrandizement as well. At the end of World War II, Yugoslav troops occupied much of Italy's Venezia Giulia around the port city of Trieste (Map 3) as well as parts of Austria's Carinthia province around Klagenfurt (Map 4). Yet, the arrival of Anglo-American occupation troops in both regions in the mid-1945 reversed the facts on the ground which

Map 3 The post–World War II territorial disputes over Venezia Giulia, Trieste, and Gorizia between Yugoslavia and Italy. The northern half of the free territory, including the city of Trieste, joined Italy in 1954.

---

[52] NZZ-m, 6/14/1946:2; BT, 6/10/1947:3; Tat, 5/15/1947:2; NZZ-m, 7/26/1947:2; CDT, 7/4/1947:9; MG, 12/30/1947:6.

Map 4 Map of the territorial disputes on parts of Carinthia (left of center) between Yugoslavia (Jugoslawien) and Austria (Österreich). Yugoslavia formally withdrew its claims in 1955.
Source: *Berner Tagwacht*, January 28, 1947, p. 2.

Tito had tried to create in the chaos of the ending war. Unsurprisingly, in the fall of 1946, Yugoslavia rejected the territorial compromises worked out at Paris Peace Conference even if it had awarded the country much of the claimed territory in Venezia Giulia *except* for the Trieste region. The formal Yugoslav occupation of the awarded parts in September of 1947 prompted thousands of Slovenes to escape to Italy. The same month, US occupation troops blocked the advance of Yugoslav units into the Trieste region. Two months later, Yugoslav troops closed all crossing points at the new border with Italy by erecting low walls across the roads to prevent any vehicular traffic.[53]

Tito's Yugoslavia similarly tried to expand its Slovenian borders northwestward into Austria. His rhetoric resonated with nationalists at home and with some among the 60,000- to 80,000-strong Slovene minority in Carinthia. However, Yugoslavia's assertive policies – including the shooting down of American planes, the stationing of troops near the border, frequent clashes with British occupation troops in Austria, and the indiscriminate killing of civilians on the Austrian side of the border in recurrent raids – undermined the country's relationship with the Anglo-American powers.[54] Before mid-1948, the USSR supported

---

[53] Robert Niebuhr, "Enlarging Yugoslavia," *European History Quarterly*, 47/2 (2017), pp. 287–91; Marina Cattaruzza, *Italy and Its Eastern Border, 1866–2016* (Routledge, 2017), pp. 192–242; *WP*, 9/21/1946:3; *DBG*, 9/17/1947:14; *Sun*, 9/17/1947:6; *Freiburger Nachrichten*, 11/7/1947:3.

[54] Niebuhr, "Enlarging Yugoslavia," pp. 291–94; *NZN*, 10/27/1945:8; *BT*, 8/13/1946:2; *Scotsman*, 12/12/1946:4; *CSM*, 12/26/1946:6; *IT*, 1/7/1947:4; *NZZ*-m, 1/23/1947:1; *NYT*, 3/28/1947:1; *Bund*-m, 7/3/1947:2.

Yugoslavia's territorial demands mainly for the purpose of delaying the Austria's State Treaty (peace treaty), which would have terminated Allied, including Soviet, occupation. In any case, Yugoslavia moderated its policy toward Austria in mid-1947 when it became evident that its territorial demands went nowhere. Even while Tito's government fortified the Slovenian–Carinthian border at that time – particularly with the stationing of trusted Serbian troops – Yugoslavia simultaneously simplified entry visa rules for foreign tourists – including Austrians.[55]

The second conference of the Cominform (the Soviet-led organization of the world's communist parties) on June 19–23, 1948, declared Yugoslavia a Marxist-Leninist heretic.[56] As the ideological conflict with the USSR had deepened over the spring of 1948, Yugoslavia started to fortify its 330-kilometer border to Austria – consisting of a flat eastern stretch and an Alpine western stretch – to prevent further escapes, particularly of political dissidents. Wherever possible, a zone adjacent to the border line was cleared of vegetation, watchtowers were erected a mile apart from each other, and cross-border roads were permanently blocked. In early August of 1948, the government in Belgrade also cancelled all passports to prevent anybody from leaving, even if holders of old passports still were allowed to return from abroad. This regime denied passports to the vast majority of Yugoslav citizens until 1959. Only Yugoslavia's Jews were allowed to emigrate to Israel on the basis of a 1948 bilateral agreement.[57]

In the wake of the split with the USSR and under threat of internal turmoil, the League of Communists in Yugoslavia purged pro-Soviet officials. Within days of introducing the new passport policy, high-ranking Yugoslav military and political leaders tried to escape by crossing illegally into Romania; some succeeded, others were shot, and yet others got arrested. In parallel, tensions increased at the borders to Yugoslavia's socialist neighbors. As early as May of 1948, the USSR had increased its troops at the short border of its Austrian occupation zone to Yugoslavia (at the flat Burgenland stretch) with a transfer of 75,000 men from Hungary (Map 4). In response, Yugoslav border guards regularly machine-gunned Soviet troops patrolling the boundary line, which eventually forced the Soviet command to evacuate the immediate border zone permanently. Soviet occupation troops in Hungary, Romania, and Bulgaria

---

[55] Gerald Stourzh and Wolfgang Mueller, *Der Kampf um den Staatsvertrag 1945–1955*, 6th, enl. ed. (Böhlau, 2020), p. 156; *NZN*, 5/21/1947:6; *NZZ*-m, 7/15/1957:5; *NZZ*-n, 7/29/1947:2; *CSM*, 8/13/1947:6; *NZZ*-m, 8/26/1947:2; *NZN*, 4/27/1948:6; *NZZ*-m, 6/4/1947:5; *NZZ*-n, 11/2/1951:10.
[56] Lorenz Lüthi, *Cold Wars* (Cambridge University Press, 2020), p. 73.
[57] *NYT*, 7/5/1948:4; *Observer*, 5/24/1959:8; *CSM*, 8/10/1948:12; *NZZ*, 12/19/1948:5.

Map 5 Map of Yugoslavia in 1953; note the Soviet divisions at the Yugoslav border, indicating the Iron Curtain between Yugoslavia and its socialist neighbors.

Source: "Iron Curtain Patrol," *Jerusalem Post*, July 15, 1953, p. 4.

(Map 5) were less visibly involved in active duty at the borders to Yugoslavia.[58] In July 1953, four months after Stalin's death, Yugoslavia and its three neighbors agreed to the creation of bilateral commissions to settle border incidents. Nikita S. Khrushchev's visit to Belgrade in May 1955 buried the Soviet–Yugoslav split, at least temporarily. In the fall, the USSR even reduced its troop presence in Hungary and Romania, following its military withdrawal

---

[58] Marie-Janine Calic, *Geschichte Jugoslawiens im 20. Jahrhundert* (C.H. Beck, 2010), pp. 189–92; *NZZ*-e, 8/18/1949:2; FOIA Reading Room: CIA-RDP63-00314R000200140016-0, p. 1; CIA-RDP82-00457R008100460006-0, CIA-RDP82-00457R007100400006-7, CIA-RDP82-00457R006300430005-4, CIA-RDP82-00457R007100260004-5; *Bund*-e, 6/3/1948:2; *WP*, 10/22/1951:9; *Bund*-e, 6/3/1948:2; *WP*, 10/22/1951:9.

from eastern Austria according to the provisions of the Austrian State Treaty of May 15, 1955.[59]

The border tensions after mid-1948 caused Yugoslavia and its three neighbors Hungary, Romania, and Bulgaria to introduce strict border regimes. The fortifications included defensive works on both sides, which sported barbed wires, watchtowers, minefields, and restricted areas further inland. In Hungary's and Romania's border areas, untrustworthy local populations – Serbs, Croats, Germans, and even Bulgarians – were removed. In some cases, like Romania's Banat, removal occurred from a border region up to 60 kilometers deep. As a result of these removals, Hungarian armed forces, for example, had to bring in the harvest in depopulated rural areas. The Yugoslav side implemented a similar policy on corresponding minorities on its side of the border; in a reflection of conflicts within in its own multiethnic population, however, it removed primarily Croats and Slovenes from the Serbian Banat. Despite all these fortifications, people still managed to cross the borders illegally, like the hundreds of Hungarian soldiers and civilians that defected to Yugoslavia in 1949.[60]

Yugoslavia's conflict with Albania, which the Soviet–Yugoslav Split aggravated up to the rupture of diplomatic relations for thirteen years, was related to Tito's long-standing attempts to control the communist party of the small Mediterranean country. The split allowed the pro-Soviet faction within the Albanian party to overthrow and expel the pro-Yugoslav faction, and even execute some of its leaders. Thus, the mountainous Yugoslav–Albanian border experienced thousands of border incidents – few of them lethal, though – and the collapse of formal economic and cross-border contacts. Most of the incidents were related to illegal border crossings – including by dissidents – and smuggling in both directions as well as intelligence and diversionary operations. In the second half of 1953 and in 1954, Belgrade and Tirana agreed on the peaceful resolution of border incidents and the renewal of border markings.[61]

Yugoslavia's tensions with its four socialist neighbors forced Tito's government to withdraw troops – as much as 80 percent – from the borders to Italy and Austria. Overall, this lessened the intensity of Yugoslavia's border conflicts with the two non-communist neighbors, but tensions still flared up from time to time, particularly in Trieste and Gorizia. In 1947, the Anglo-American Allies had decided to divide the Trieste region temporarily into two zones under Allied control – Zone A

---

[59] FOIA Reading Room: CIA-RDP80-00809A000700060259-7, CIA-RDP80-00809A0007000903 42-1, CIA-RDP80-00809A000700100210-5; *NZZ*-n, 7/3/1953:2; *NYT*, 7/12/1953:17; *NYT*, 7/20/1953:6; Lüthi, *Cold Wars*, pp. 77–78; *NZZ*-m, 8/1/1955:5.
[60] Distilled from several dozens of documents from: FOIA Reading Room.
[61] Elidor Mëhilli, *From Stalin to Mao* (Cornell University Press, 2018), pp. 45–53; Marko B. Miletic, "Incidenti na granicama između Jugoslavije i zemalja Informbiroa (1948–1955)," *Tokovi Istorijie*, 2 (2020), pp. 185–208.

with Trieste itself and Zone B to the south encompassing the northwestern part of the Istrian peninsula. The purpose was to let nationalist passions on both sides cool down before making a final decision on the future of the region. In daily life, however, the two zones de facto integrated into Italy and Yugoslavia.[62]

Further north, the 232-kilometer-long Italian-Yugoslav border line divided the city of Gorizia into a larger Italian section and a smaller Yugoslav part, separated by a narrow urban strip lined with Yugoslav armed guards and barbed wire. By 1949, the guards mostly prevented escapees from leaving illegally, occasionally shooting and killing some. An attempt in 1950 to regulate local border traffic for urban residents from both parts of the city ended in chaos when 5,000 Yugoslav citizens broke through the barricades to escape to relatives on the Italian side. In any case, the urban entanglement of divided Gorizia always allowed for individual escapes at any moment, as did the open Adriatic Sea further south. In the context of declining border tensions with its socialist neighbors, however, Yugoslavia eventually signed an agreement on October 5, 1954, with the Anglo-American powers and with Italy that made the division of the Trieste region permanent.[63]

Yugoslavia's disputes with Austria similarly diminished over the 1948–55 period. In the wake of the Yugoslav passport cancellation in August 1948, the border still remained a major place of illegal escapes – including by politicians from Yugoslavia and other socialist states. By 1950, the Yugoslav border service routinely shot dead illegal border crossers, although it simultaneously improved cooperation with its Austrian counterpart. Regardless, Yugoslavia's territorial demands continued to block the conclusion of an Austrian State Treaty, even if Belgrade unilaterally ended the state of war with Austria in a sign of goodwill in early 1951. As the result of Yugoslavia's gradual reduction of border guards, violent incidents declined as well. In 1951, 60–80 persons still crossed illegally into Austria every month.[64] A major breakthrough in the difficult relationship occurred during the seminal visit of Austria's foreign minister to Yugoslavia in June 1952. In its wake, the two countries signed a local border agreement that allowed the resumption of economic and personal contacts. On May 15, 1955, Yugoslavia formally dropped its territorial claims on Carinthia and announced its intention to sign the Austrian State Treaty, which the Allied Powers and Austria concluded that very day.[65]

---

[62] Massimo Bucarelli, "The Adriatic Section of the Iron Curtain," Martin Previšić, ed., *Rethinking the Cold War* (De Gruyter, 2021), pp. 171–77.

[63] *DBG*, 7/10/1949:C15; *Bieler Tagblatt*, 8/14/1950:3; *NZZ*-e, 10/10/1950:6; *NZZ*-e, 8/21/1950:2; *NZZ*-m, 1/12/1952:2; *NZZ*-e, 2/21/1952:2; *NZZ*-e, 6/27/1952:2; *NZZ*-e, 10/5/1954:5.

[64] *SCMP*, 1/110/1949:7; FOIA Reading Room: CIA-RDP82-00457R005300450001-7, CIA-RDP82-00457R005400690012-8; *NYT*, 6/4/1949:5; *Bund*-m, 10/4/1950:2; *SCSP-Herald*, 1/21/1951:5; *CSM*, 3/20/1951:3.

[65] Maximilian Graf and Petra Mayrhofer, "Austria and Yugoslavia in the Cold War," Previšić, *Rethinking*, p. 155; *NZZ*-m, 9/11/1952:1; *Bund*-e, 5/15/1955:2.

Unlike the other parts of Churchill's Iron Curtain after 1955, as described in further sections, Yugoslavia's mostly pacified borders to its two non-communist neighbors experienced no longer high volumes of escapes or much violence for the remainder of the Cold War. Only occasionally, the numbers of Yugoslav refugees slipping across the border to Austria reached over a 1,000 per month. Border crossing still remained a criminal offense for a long time, and border guards occasionally killed escapees. Yet, refugees more likely faced death in crossing dangerous Alpine terrain during inclement weather conditions.[66] Starting in 1957, Yugoslavia considered and then de facto allowed labor emigration to the non-socialist world in order to undercut illegal exits. And in August of 1959, Yugoslavia lifted the strict passport regime to allow travel abroad, including emigration. By then, according to its own statistics, around 200,000 Yugoslav citizens had illegally left since 1948. In 1965, eventually, the country reduced the restricted areas at most of its entire land border from 15 kilometers to a zone of a few hundred meters.[67]

4 Hungary's Iron Curtain, 1945–1955

Hungary was East Europe's first socialist country to lower the Iron Curtain at its 356-kilometer-long western border to Austria. From the end of World War II to September 15, 1947, when the seven-month-old Paris Peace Treaty entered force, Hungary's western border technically remained under Soviet-American-British-French Allied control. Until the withdrawal of all Allied occupation forces from Austria in October of 1955, Hungary also was an important staging ground for Soviet troops stationed beyond its western border in eastern Austria (Map 6).[68]

The immediate post–World War II period laid the political and organizational groundwork for the Iron Curtain at Hungary's western border. Within three years, the Soviet military occupation administration skillfully manipulated the Hungarian political system to elevate the communist party, which had lost the free parliamentary elections in November 1945, into a position of political dominance. In the first half of 1947, leading non-communist politicians were arrested, imprisoned, or even deported to the USSR. By late May, the Hungarian Communist Party also removed the non-communist prime minister during his official visit to Switzerland, taking the last step to assume complete power.

---

[66] *JP*, 8/18/1957:1; *Sun*, 12/7/1964:2; *CDT*, 7/3/1961:B5; *HC*, 6/19/1958:6; *CDT*, 10/31/1959:8.
[67] *CSM*, 8/29/1957:3; *CSM*, 8/10/1948:12; *NZZ*-e, 7/14/1961:5; also: www.eiserner-vorhang.de/grenzregime/08_Jugoslawien/index.html, accessed December 12, 2024.
[68] István Orgoványi, "Menekülés a Vasfüggönyön át Tiltott határátlépések 1945 és 1950 között," *Betekintő*, 1 (2017), p. 9.

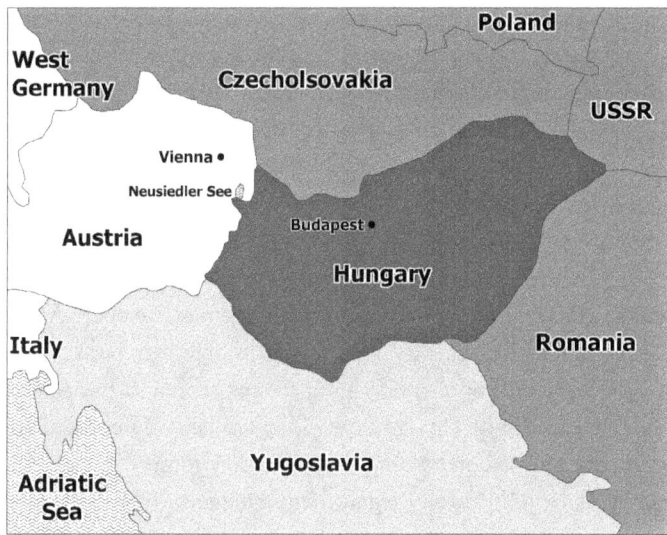

Map 6 During the Cold War, Hungary fortified its borders to Austria, Yugoslavia, and Romania.

Since he and diplomats stationed abroad refused to return home, the new communist-dominated government simply denaturalized them.[69]

In early June of 1947, Hungarian citizens started to flee to Vienna to escape purges and arrests. Beginning in August, Hungarian border guards turned apprehended border crossers over to the court system for sentencing as de facto offenders. But only on November 15, 1947, did Hungary close its borders completely. Radio Moscow announced that Budapest had created a 15-kilometer-deep border area to prevent the escape of "political refugees." Yet, Hungarians continued to stream out of the country across the poorly guarded border during all of 1948. Most did not stop in Vienna but moved surreptitiously through the Soviet zone of occupation in Austria to the American zone, and then even beyond.[70]

Originally, Hungary's postwar government had allowed citizens to visit Austria with a newly – but rarely – issued passport. However, until September of 1947, Soviet occupation authorities retained the monopoly on issuing exit visas. Permanent residents of border districts still received special identification

---

[69] Mária Palasik, *Chess Game for Democracy* (McGill-Queen's University Press, 2011); *MG*, 5/30/1947:8; *SCMP*, 6/7/1947:7.

[70] Károly Kókai, "Ungarische Migrationswellen, 1945–1963," Csaba Szabó, ed., *Österreich und Ungarn im 20. Jahrhundert* (Institut für Ungarische Geschichtsforschung in Wien, 2014), pp. 245–49; György Nagy, "A Magyar Állami Határrendőrség létrehozásának körülményei, szervezetei, 1945–1949 között," *Határőrségi Tanulmányok*, 5 (1999), no page numbers; *NYT*, 11/26/1947:4; *Bieler Tagblatt*, 11/28/1947:2 (quote); *Bund*-e, 2/25/1948:1; *NZZ*-n, 2/26/1948:2; *NZZ*-n, 10/14/1948:2; *NZZ*-n, 12/3/1948:2; *NZZ*-e, 1/10/1949:2.

cards to cross the border into corresponding Austrian districts to maintain customary relations. But Hungarians had little reason to visit or even move to Austria, since economic life in their own country before communist takeover in mid-1947 was better than in the four-power-occupied and starving neighbor to the West. The only exceptions to this strict border regime affected ethnic Germans and Jews expelled from East Europe. Both groups crossed the border without much paperwork and even in coordination with the four Allies.[71]

In the immediate postwar years, Hungarian border guards were understaffed to deal with the massive population movements in either direction. Although the postwar government had quickly resurrected its interwar border services, it initially could only rely on a small number of experienced but aging guards. Poorly equipped and limited in size by the 1945 armistice agreement, the border guards primarily focused on fighting organized smuggling.[72]

Starting in late 1947, Hungary significantly tightened its border regime, both legally and physically. In the context of the unfolding Cold War and the developing Soviet–Yugoslav Split, Hungary's communist party accepted Soviet notions of inherent East–West hostility. As a consequence, the government in Budapest introduced Soviet models of passport regulations, border control, and weapons systems, including the creation of a State Defense Authority. In late 1947, Hungary even began to fortify its western border to Austria and soon thereafter its southern border to Yugoslavia with wire fences, watchtowers, minefields, and the clearing of a 50-meter-wide zone along the border. Late in 1948, the zone to Austria had grown to 300 meters; by mid-1949, it even reached up to one kilometer at various places. Settlements lying within were forcefully removed.[73]

In parallel to the fortification of the actual boundary line, Hungary also established a 15-kilometer-wide border area with controlled access and restricted residence regulations. Starting in 1948, Hungarian police forces monitored train and private car traffic towards the border to catch potential refugees. Soviet manpower significantly supported the understaffed Hungarian border guards in the early period until its transfer to the borders with Yugoslavia (see Section 3). Despite the change of Hungary's focus toward its southern border after mid-1948, the stream of refugees to Austria still fell to a trickle by

---

[71] Orgoványi, "Menekülés," pp. 1, 3; Péter Bencsik and Nagy György, *A magyar úti okmányok története 1945–89* (Tipico Design Kft., 2005), pp. 12, 14; *BT*, 6/27/1947:1.

[72] László Gáspár, "A második világháború utáni magyar határőrizet változásai," *Acta Historiae Praesidii Ordinis*, 22 (2012), pp. 32–35; Orgoványi, "Menekülés," p. 3.

[73] Gáspár, "A második," pp. 36–40; Orgoványi, "Menekülés," p. 14; Lajos Gecsenyi, *"Die Beziehungen zwischen Ungarn und Österreich, 1945–1964,"* Heeresgeschichtliches Museum Wien, *Der Eiserne Vorhang* (Heeresgeschichtliches Museum, 2001), pp. 54, 83; *NZZ*-e, 12/13/1948:2; *NZZ*, 5/12/1949:8.

March 1949. Hungarian border fortifications continued to be updated on a regular basis in the first half of the 1950s.[74]

Also in 1948, the Hungarian government tightened legal measures to deter escapes. Illegal border crossings in both directions, including assistance and the provision of fake papers, became punishable with up to five years in prison. However, transgressors could significantly lower their sentences if they turned themselves in to Hungarian authorities, which, of course, only occurred in cases of illegal entry. These strict legal measures remained on the books until 1961. Hence, by 1949, the Hungarian government had made the legal exit of citizens virtually impossible. The previous year, it also had cancelled identification cards for permanent residents in border districts, tearing apart historical ties between neighboring communities.[75]

As a result of the fortification of the border to Austria since the late 1940s, the number of casualties increased, though no official or verified statistics have surfaced. Refugees were shot by machine gun fire or blown up by mines. Hungarian border guards themselves stepped on poorly marked mines, as did wildlife that had settled in the border zone. Austrian border guards were killed by their Hungarian counterparts in recurring firefights that sometimes transpired on Austrian territory. Bullets of Hungarian border guards regularly hit Austrian territory hundreds of meters from the border. Mine shrapnel and gun shots hurt and killed Austrian farmers working on fields and vineyards close to the border. Rainstorms washed mines onto Austrian territory where they exploded unexpectedly.[76] Starting in October 1949, the Austrian government filed protests with its Hungarian counterpart – to no avail. The ideologically phrased replies asserted that the border fortifications primarily were in place to prevent fascists and American spies from entering Hungary.[77]

The complete sealing of the borders allowed Hungarians – entrepreneurs and likely even officials – to monopolize smuggling to the Soviet-occupied zone of Austria, often in cooperation with Soviet troops stationed on both sides of border. Austrian businesses faced a double problem; they had lost their external market in East Europe in 1945 and now were competing against discount

---

[74] Gecsenyi, "Beziehungen," pp. 54, 83; *Tat*, 2/2/1951:2; Orgoványi, "Menekülés," p. 22; FOIA Reading Room: CIA-RDP82-00457R004300230011-1, CIA-RDP80-00809A000500820301-3; *Bund*-m, 3/30/1949:1; Eva Varga, "Technische und mentalitätsgeschichtliche Aspekte des Eisernen Vorhangs an der österreichisch-ungarischen Grenze 1949–1956," Peter Haslinger, ed., *Grenze im Kopf* (Peter Lang, 1999), p. 116.

[75] Orgoványi, "Menekülés," pp. 13, 20–21; Bencsik/Nagy, *A magyar úti okmányok története*, p. 20; Varga, "Technische und mentalitätsgeschichtliche Aspekte," p. 117.

[76] Varga, "Technische und mentalitätsgeschichtliche Aspekte," p. 116; *Bund*-m, 8/3/1949:2; *HT*, 8/4/1949:5; *NZZ*-m, 9/29/1949:2; *Bund*-m, 1/25/1950:1; *BT*, 3/11/1950:2; *NZZ*-n, 5/15/1950:2; Szorger/Bayer, *Burgenland*, p. 7.

[77] *NZZ*-n, 10/20/1949:2; *Bund*-m, 11/29/1949:2; *Tat*, 10/21/1949:1.

contraband from behind the Iron Curtain. The contraband even included paying refugees shipped across the border hidden in Soviet army trucks.[78]

But what was the purpose of the heavily fortified border lines? The border regime primarily served the overall goal of the government to control and regulate the life of the country's population.[79] In the initial period after mid-1947, the Hungarian communists tried to arrest non-communist politicians in purges at home and to prevent them from leaving and organizing abroad. Economic needs to retain labor, however, seemed not to have played a major role. Hungary did not suffer a great loss of population – that is, labor – during and after World War II, in contrast to the USSR, Czechoslovakia, and East Germany, as described in other sections.

Even after 1948, Hungarians still found ways to flee. Some escaped to Yugoslavia as long as it was still possible. Others managed to navigate the minefields on the border to Austria, including laying planks across them. Even numerous Hungarian border guards decided to flee; they knew weaknesses in the border regime from daily routine. Yet, other refugees used self-made armored cars to crash through the border fortifications. Swimmers absconded through the *Neusiedler See* – the large border lake between Hungary and Austria. A family escaped hiding in a train freight car. As the ever-improving border fortifications made escapes more difficult, black market prices for guided escapes increased in the early 1950s.[80] Greater vigilance by Hungarian authorities in a region of 30–50 kilometers inside the border also meant that refugees often arrived in Austria only with the set of clothes they were wearing as their only possessions. Hand-carried luggage of any sort would have aroused suspicion on the way to the border. Even a successful escape did not mean that refugees were safe in the Soviet-occupied part of Austria before Soviet withdrawal in October 1955, which is why many tried to reach the British or American zones. Earlier that year, for example, Soviet troops had collected an escaped family, which had been shot and wounded, from their hospital beds in the Soviet zone of Austria and sent them back to Hungary.[81]

5 Czechoslovakia's Iron Curtain, 1945–1955

Czechoslovakia followed Hungary's lowering of the Iron Curtain within less than a year. Even before the pro-Soviet coup in late February 1948, the country's government had already significantly restricted the right of foreign travel by its

---

[78] *NYT*, 1/19/1949:8; *Bund*-m, 8/3/1949:2.   [79] Gáspár, "A második," p. 39.
[80] FOIA Reading Room: CIA-RDP82-00457R002600620010-8; *HT*, 8/4/1949:5; *JP*, 9/24/1950:4; *Tat*, 10/21/1949:1; FOIA Reading Room: CIA-RDP82-00457R003800570008-4; *WP*, 12/15/1955:4; *CDT*, 10/28/1952:38; *MG*, 7/28/1949:5; *JP*, 8/24/1950:4; *AS*, 4/10/1952:A16.
[81] *NYT*, 8/17/1953:14; *DBG*, 11/18/1951:C1; *Tat*, 4/4/1955:2.

citizens for almost three years. The post–World War II expulsion of ethnic Germans from the areas along its entire western border – 454 kilometers to the Soviet zone of occupation in Germany, 357 kilometers to the American zone of occupation, and 573 kilometers to Austria – had led to the creation of unique thinly populated boundary area (Map 7). On the surface, Czechoslovakia's early Iron Curtain seemed to resemble its Hungarian counterpart, but in reality had different political and domestic causes.

Czechoslovakia's borders to Germany and Austria had remained open for a few years after the end of World War II, though not for the majority of its own citizens. Jewish emigration and Jewish transit, primarily from Poland to Vienna, continued into the late 1940s.[82] From the late spring of 1945 to the fall of 1946, Czechoslovakia also expelled a large share of its ethnic German minority – the *Sudetendeutsche* – from the borderlands. Since the Nazi regime had used them as a Trojan horse to occupy the Czech part of the country in 1938–39, the postwar Czechoslovak government unsurprisingly considered the German minority a security threat. After a violent and improvised start in June of 1945 that led to the chaotic departure of 700,000–800,000 *Sudetendeutsche*,

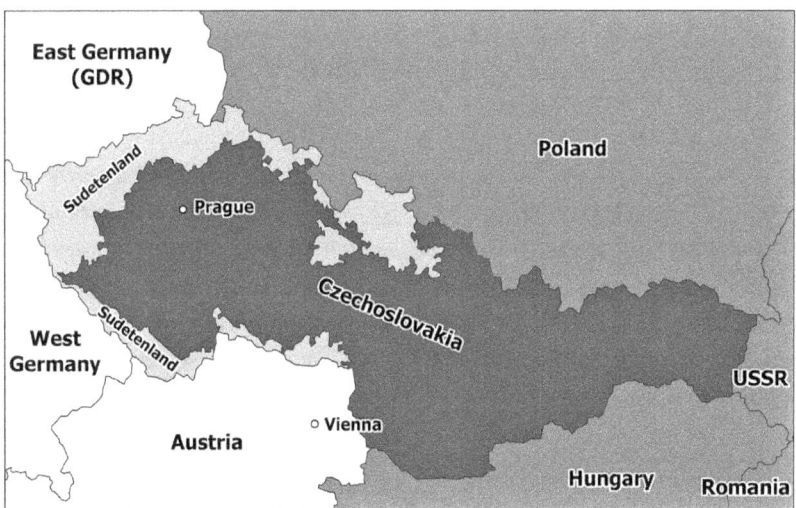

Map 7 Post–World War II Czechoslovakia lost its eastern tip to the USSR. The country expelled its *Sudetendeutsche* (ethnic German) population from borderlands (Sudetenland) in the Czech part, and its Hungarian population from the Slovak part in 1945–46.

---

[82] *BT*, 7/17/1946:3; *NZZ*-m, 2/13/1947:2.

Czechoslovak–Allied cooperation after August resulted in a more orderly transfer of 750,000 *Sudetendeutsche* to the Soviet occupation zone of Germany and 2.5 million to the American zone (primarily Bavaria) within fourteen months. Still, around 200,000–300,000 skilled workers vital to glass, textile, mining, and other industries were allowed to stay. In total, Czechoslovakia lost over a quarter of its population after the spring of 1945, including Jews and Hungarians. Despite policies to settle Czechs and Slovaks in the former German borderlands, this massive loss of people left much of the former *Sudetenland* thinly populated for decades to come.[83]

Since the end of the war, Czechoslovak citizens had not been allowed to leave the country for private travel or emigration. Even if they theoretically enjoyed the right to obtain a passport, they rarely received one. The elected three-party communist/socialist coalition government of the immediate postwar period justified this practice on the basis of lack of foreign currency reserves to provide valuta to travelers, national economic needs (shortage of labor), and general security interests. While travel restrictions to the former enemy countries Germany, Austria, and Hungary were understandable, the regulations also applied to travel to Poland. However, local border traffic to Poland, Hungary, and Austria remained legal into the early 1950s, but was prohibited to both the Soviet zone of occupation in East Germany and the American zone of occupation in West Germany, largely for the purpose of cutting residual cross-border ties or preventing new ones from forming.[84]

Until early 1948, Czechoslovakia's borders to Germany and Austria remained both poorly guarded and hardly fortified. Border guards lacked equipment and personnel, which led to significant smuggling activities. Over the course of the first three postwar years, the Czechoslovak government closed progressively a number of border crossing points to prevent the illegal exit of Nazi collaborators. Still, the forested and hilly German–Czechoslovak border areas served as a conduit for continued illegal exit and entry, including by secret services and political infiltrators, in both directions. By early 1947, Czechoslovakia

---

[83] David W. Gerlach, *The Economy of Ethnic Cleansing* (Cambridge University Press, 2017), pp. 1–18, 33–39, 53–64, 78–85; Niklas Perzi, "Leben am und mit dem Eisernen Vorhang," Technical Museum Brno, ed., *Der Eiserne Vorhang, 1948–1989* (Technické muzeum, 2019), p. 108; Markus A. Meinke, "Die Entwicklung der tschechoslowakischen Grenzsicherung an der Landesgrenze zu Bayern 1945 bis 1970," Markus A. Meinke, *Die Entwicklung der tschechoslowakischen Grenzsicherung* (Regensburger Hefte zur Geschichte und Kultur im östlichen Europa, 2007), pp. 8–12.

[84] Jan Rychlík, *Cestování do ciziny v habsburské monarchii a v Ceskoslovensku* (Ústav pro soudobé dějiny AV ČR, 2007), pp. 26–33; Tomáš Jílek, "Spezifika der Bewachung der tschechisch-bayerischen Staatsgrenze zu Zeiten des 'Eisernen Vorhangs' 1948–1989," Markus A. Meinke, *Die tschechisch-bayerische Grenze im Kalten Krieg in vergleichender Perspektive* (Stadtarchiv Regensburg, 2011), pp. 47–48.

eventually established a 5-kilometer-wide, uninhabited area at some stretches of its border to Bavaria. In the same year, it also launched a two-year-long policy of dispersing the remnant *Sudetendeutsche* population throughout the country.[85]

The communist takeover in Hungary in late May 1947 and the subsequent one-year-long development of the Soviet–Yugoslav Split served as a portent for the Soviet-supported communist coup in Czechoslovakia on February 21–25, 1948. Already during the coup itself, the communist-dominated Interior Ministry closed the borders, replaced regular border and custom officials with units of the *Sbor národní bezpečnosti* (SNP; National Security Corps), and introduced even stricter exit visa regulations. Within days, a stream of refugees – mostly politically persecuted citizens as well as *Sudetendeutsche* – started to cross illegally the borders to the American zones of occupation in Germany and Austria. Overwhelmed, SNB troops requested backup, but to no avail. The central government instead tried to control the access roads to the border areas to block escapes of political enemies who could engage in anti-communist agitation in exile. Citizens who were apprehended while trying to exit received uniform prison sentences of five years. According to US news reports, 60 percent of refugees got caught in the period to late 1948, amounting to 45,000 individuals convicted to prison. Among those who succeeded in escaping were 61 members of parliament, 9 former ministers, 6 generals, and 600 army officers. Even if there was no formal shoot-to-kill order, border guards routinely killed refugees without warning – the first lethal case occurred on March 11, 1948.[86]

The physical self-isolation of the newly established, pro-Soviet Czechoslovak Socialist Republic (CSSR) from the Western world progressively continued over the following four years. During the remainder of 1948, the SNB erected a simple barbed wire fence with a series of wooden watchtowers along its borders to Bavaria and Austria. In October, the communist government voided the right to a passport by its citizens. Within yet another month, the Interior Ministry decided to introduce a new, dedicated border service to start serving on January 1, 1949. With Soviet advice and material support, it replaced the one-year-old, barbed wire fences with a plowed strip, trip wires, minefields, three rows of 5,000-volt electrical fences, watchtowers, and earthen bunkers. Further inland,

---

[85] Meinke, "Die Entwicklung der tschechoslowakischen Grenzsicherung," pp. 12–15; Perzi, "Leben," p. 109; Prokop Tomek, "Grenzübertritte der Grenzgängeragenten und Kuriere," Technical Museum Brno, *Eiserne Vorhang*, pp. 41–43; Jílek, "Spezifika," p. 48; David Kovařík, "Zwangsmigration nahe der Tschechoslowakischen Staatsgrenze während des Kalten Krieges," Technical Museum Brno, ed., *Der Eiserne Vorhang, 1948–1989* (Technické muzeum, 2019), p. 85.

[86] Rychlík, *Cestování do ciziny*, pp. 34, 47–48; Jílek, "Spezifika," pp. 48–49; *Tat*, 3/4/1948:2; Meinke, "Entwicklung," p. 18; *CSM*, 12/16/1948:14.

the ministry established a restricted-access border area from which most residents were removed. In September of 1949, the government also ordered an exchange of all passports, although the policy primarily aimed at reducing the number of holders drastically and thereby decreasing continued foreign travel, even on official missions. Later that year, a nightly curfew closed all border crossing points to the Western world.[87]

In July 1951, Czechoslovakia once more tightened its border regime to West Germany and Austria, but did not introduce similar measures at its borders to Poland and Hungary. The Soviet-style National Security Ministry, which had been created a little more than a year before, was put in charge of protecting the state borders with 3,000 professional soldiers and 13,500 conscripts. The actual border zone was uniformly extended to 2,000 meters, was cleared of all inhabitants, and remained inaccessible to anybody except the border service. A border area of 6–8 kilometers and a border region of ten to twenty kilometers further inland secured control of access and the detention of potential refugees. Apprehended refugees received prison sentences for up to five years, carriers of state secrets even much higher punishments.[88]

In the same month, the National Security Ministry also issued an *explicit* shoot-to-kill permission in cases where border violators could not be stopped otherwise, but simultaneously prohibited shooting across the border line into a neighboring country.[89] Only days before, Czechoslovak border guards had killed a West German border guard with a burst of machine gun fire across the border line. The following year, the ministry once more ordered the further fortification of the border. Most of the residents from within a 10-kilometer-wide area were forcefully removed, while all local cross-border traffic was completely terminated. At the same time, the CSSR also formally restricted the issuance of passports exclusively to members of official missions traveling abroad. And in mid-1953, it eventually started to implement corresponding security measures at its borders to East Germany in order to prevent escapes by Czechoslovak citizens through East Berlin to West Berlin, which after mid-1952 had become the major route for refugees, as described in the next section.[90]

---

[87] Meinke, "Entwicklung," pp. 19–21; Rychlík, *Cestování do ciziny*, pp. 35, 38; Jílek, "Spezifika," p. 49; *Bund*-m, 9/21/1949:1; *Tat*, 10/21/1949:1; *Bund*-e, 12/19/1949:1; *WP*, 11/12/1949:2.

[88] Rychlík, *Cestování do ciziny*, pp. 39, 41; Martin Pulec, "Die Opfer der militärischen Bewachung der Staatsgrenze in den Sechzigerjahren des 20. Jahrhunderts," Technical Museum Brno, *Eiserne Vorhang*, pp. 51–52; Jílek, "Spezifika," p. 51; FOIA reading room: CIA-RDP82-00457R007800150003-4; Meinke, "Entwicklung," pp. 23–26.

[89] Meinke, "Entwicklung," pp. 24–25.

[90] *Tat*, 7/6/1951:2; Tomáš Slavík, "Pioniertechnische Grenzsicherungsanlagen," Technical Museum Brno, *Eiserne Vorhang*, pp. 63–82; Pavel Vaněk, "Die Bewachung der Staatsgrenzen und die Grenzwacht," Technical Museum Brno, *Eiserne Vorhang*, pp. 23, 30; Rychlík, *Cestování*

The ever-tightening border measures did not prevent all escapes. Western news media reported that, by mid-1950, 400 persons on average still managed to flee every month to West Germany and Austria. A few, among them former Czechoslovak pilots from the Royal Air Force, used airplanes; but most fled by land. Refugees paid guides who helped them to escape. Armored trucks managed to crash through barriers; if they failed, their occupants returned gunfire to ensure a successful escape. A train with intentionally disabled emergency brakes rushed through a border station to Bavaria; of the 109 people on board, 38 applied for asylum while the rest decided to return. Until the fall of 1955, fleeing to the Soviet-occupied part of Austria ran the additional risk of being arrested by Soviet occupation troops, which sent those caught back to the CSSR.[91]

In the period of Czechoslovakia's fortified borders from late 1948 to late 1989, over 171,000 people left the country without permit (though not exclusively via crossing the border illegally) and almost 49,000 were arrested attempting to do so. At least 281 died in the attempt, of whom 145 were shot, 96 electrocuted by the 5,000-volt electrical fences, 16 committed suicide after arrest, 11 drowned, and the remaining 13 perished of various reasons. Another 50 bodies washed up in border rivers on the Austrian side. At least 584 border guards died – 243 in accidents, 185 of suicide, the remaining 156 of gun fights with deserters or border crossers, or due to other causes.[92] Once in a while, Western border guards helplessly witnessed the pursuit and killing of refugees on the other side of the border. In October 1952, for example, Austrian officials observed over a period of 24 hours – mostly by listening to the sound of gun shots – the hunting down of 15 refugees; at its end, seven had been shot, seven were arrested, and one was missing.[93]

After the successive deaths of Stalin and the Czechoslovak communist leader Klement Gottwald within ten days in March of 1953, the communist government in Prague slightly relaxed its strict travel policies. In 1954–55, it increased the number of exit and entry visas granted, particularly with regard to travel to and from other socialist countries (except Yugoslavia). Apart from dissolving the Soviet-inspired National Security Ministry in 1953, however, no political

---

do ciziny, pp. 40–41; Perzi, "Leben," p. 111; Kovařík, "Zwangsmigration," pp. 88–90; FOIA Reading room: CIA-RDP80-00810A006700080001-2.

[91] *WP*, 6/18/1950:M3; *NZZ*-e, 2/15/1949:2; *NZZ*-n, 3/14/1949:2; *NZZ*-e, 4/20/1940:2; *NZZ*-e, 4/27/1949:2; *JP*, 8/24/1940:4; *LAT*, 10/15/1950:G9; Markus A. Meinke, "Zweimal 'Eiserner Vorhang'? Die tschechoslowakisch-bayerische Grenze in vergleichender Perspektive zur innerdeutschen Grenze," Markus A. Meinke, *Die tschechisch-bayerische Grenze im Kalten Krieg in vergleichender Perspektive: Politische, ökonomische und soziokulturelle Dimensionen* (Stadtarchiv Regensburg, 2011), p. 56; *NYT*, 10/18/1951:15; *NZZ*-n, 1/3/1950:2; *LAT*, 10/15/1950:G9.

[92] Roman Řezníček, Pavel Vaněk, and Franz Pötscher, "Zur Einleitung," Technical Museum Brno, *Eiserne Vorhang*, p. 18.

[93] *Bieler Tagblatt*, 10/23/1952:2.

thaw similar to the concurrent Soviet one under Khrushchev occurred. On the contrary, the ongoing fortification of the border continued to completion by mid-1953. Only one border crossing point between Austria and the CSSR remained open by February 1954. Per month, a mere one hundred Czechoslovaks and one hundred Austrians crossed it in either direction, largely because Prague was restrictive in issuing entry visas while Vienna retaliated by issuing only a reciprocal number of permits.[94]

Despite, or maybe because of, the heavily fortified and armed border, incidents continued to occur. After mid-1953, Czechoslovak border guards recurrently pursued refugees into Austrian or West German territory, in violation of their own rules. Sometimes, they engaged in gun fights with Western border guards or even with American occupation troops. This still did not prevent spectacular escapes. In late July 1953, an armored, caterpillar-like vehicle with eight people crashed through the border fortifications. And airplanes still escaped unnoticed.[95] In general, however, successful escapes had become more difficult. As the mid-1950s approached, the western borders of Czechoslovakia and Hungary looked alike – a zone with barbed wire, electrical fences or minefields, a line of watchtowers, and a parallel border area which was depopulated and controlled to prevent access by possible refugees.

6 East Germany's Iron Curtain, 1945–1955

East Germany's 1,393-kilometer-long border to West Germany is among the best researched stretches of the Iron Curtain. During the first decade of the Cold War, the German–German Cold War border was not an external state border but the boundary line between the Soviet zone of occupation in Germany and its Anglo-American counterparts to the west and southwest. Germany had emerged from World War II reduced in size and divided into four occupation zones – one each by the Americans, British, Soviets, and French. Its capital was equally divided into four Allied occupation sectors but was lying entirely within the Soviet zone (Map 8). Inter-Allied agreements guaranteed free Western access (transit) to their occupation sectors, aka West Berlin, by road, rail, water, and air. Despite this territorial entanglement, the borders between the Soviet and the Anglo-American zones of Germany gradually hardened from 1945 to 1952. In comparison, zonal borders within Austria always remained relatively open. When Allied withdrawal allowed Austria to reemerge as a

---

[94] Rychlík, *Cestování do ciziny*, pp. 53–54; Meinke, "Entwicklung," pp. 27–28; *NZZ*, 7/26/1953:6; *NZZ*-m, 2/25/1954:5.
[95] Meinke, "Entwicklung," p. 28; *NZN*, 10/22/1953:6; *NZZ*-m, 12/12/1953:9; *Bund*-m, 9/16/1954:2; *NZZ*-m, 12/12/1954:2; Meinke, "Zweimal," p. 64; *DBG*, 7/26/1953:C32; *BT*, 5/13/1954:8.

Map 8 This US Army map from 1945 shows the loss of German territory in the east and the division of the remainder into four occupation zones. Divided Berlin lies in the Soviet zone. The map was published in Germany in 1945 under license from the US military government.

Source: https://commons.m.wikimedia.org/wiki/File:1945_Deutschland-Karte-der-Besatzungszonen.jpg, accessed on September 15, 2025.

sovereign and unified country in the fall of 1955, Germany, however, had become divided along the fortified Soviet–Anglo-American zonal border, although Berlin still functioned as one urban unit.[96]

Initially, the border between the Soviet and the Anglo-American occupation zones in Germany had remained open for over a year after surrender on May 8, 1945, as ethnic German expellees, refugees of all kinds, displaced persons, decommissioned soldiers, and returning evacuees crossed in both directions. NKVD troops guarded the line until late 1946. On Soviet request, the four-power Allied Control Council of Germany decided on June 30, 1946, to close the zonal border. The USSR reportedly feared a loss of qualified labor, while the Western powers were anxious to limit the uncontrolled arrival of millions of

---

[96] Flemming, *Berliner Mauer*, p. 44; Wieland Führ, *Berliner Mauer und innerdeutsche Grenze, 1945–1990* (Imhof, 2008), p. 7.

expellees and refugees. Soon thereafter, crossing the boundary was again possible but only with an interzonal passport. A few defined crossing points channeled interzonal traffic, while special identification cards allowed local cross-border traffic along the entire boundary line. On November 18, 1946, the Soviet Military Administration of Germany established the East German border police in its occupation zone, following the creation of similar forces in the American, British, and French zones. The purpose was to prevent illegal border crossings, to suppress smuggling, and to catch fleeing war criminals and Nazis. The newly created border police was highly effective; in 1947 alone, for example, it stopped 165,000 illegal exit attempts at the Soviet–American (Thuringian–Bavarian) border.[97]

In mid-1948, the Iron Curtain descended upon Germany as well, but only for goods and not for persons. The Soviet blockade of West Berlin barred the delivery of food, commodities, and fuel not only from the surrounding Soviet occupation zone but also from the Anglo-American zones by train, road, and water through the Soviet zone. In response to the Soviet attempt to starve West Berlin into political submission, the Western powers established the famous airlift to feed and power the western half of the German capital for over a year. However, residents there still could cross the sectoral border to East Berlin and the zonal border to East Germany; individuals and organized groups engaged in smuggling on a massive scale, filling the substantial shortfalls that even the famous airlift could not alleviate. The Anglo-American powers replied to the Soviet challenge with a counterblockade of East Germany, incurring massive economic distress in the Soviet zone. Even after the Soviet lifting of the blockade in May 1949, interzonal trade remained circumscribed, largely due to the Western embargo of trade in high-technology products and other goods. In the end, the Anglo-American powers were partially co-responsible for the hardening of the Iron Curtain in Germany.[98]

Until the parallel formation of the Federal Republic of Germany (West Germany) in the three Western occupation zones and the establishment of the German Democratic Republic (GDR; communist East Germany) in the Soviet zone in 1949, almost 900,000 residents and around 1.5 million expellees from East Europe arrived from the Soviet occupation zone as refugees in West Germany. A significant number of the exiting East German residents originally had been expellees themselves. Another 650,000 persons escaped the GDR

---

[97] Rottman/Taylor, *Berlin Wall*, p. 42; Führ, *Berliner Mauer*, pp. 26–31; Thorsten Dietrich, "Die Grenzpolizei der SBZ/DDR (1946–1961)," Thorsten Dietrich, Hans Ehlert, and Rüdiger Wenzke, eds., *Im Dienste der Partei* (Ch. Links, 1998), p. 202.

[98] "[SED analysis on US-UK blockade]," [3/17/1949], *Bundesarchiv Lichterfelde*, DL 2/1662, pp. 188–190; Michael Kubina, *Ulbrichts Scheitern* (Ch. Links, 2013), pp. 56–58.

between its foundation in October 1949 and May 1955. Among the motivations to leave were political repression and dissatisfaction with the economic situation in general, but also the persecution of individuals like business owners, landowners, and non-communist politicians. Unlike Hungarians or Czechoslovaks, East Germans could escape to another part of their nation with shared linguistic and cultural traits. With the administrative and political division of Berlin in late 1948 during the Soviet blockade, the western half of the capital equally became a magnet for refugees from the communist-dominated governments in the city's other half and in East Germany.[99]

After June 30, 1946, the illegal exit across the German zonal borders had primarily constituted a violation of Allied regulations, which seemed not to have been prosecuted systematically beyond arrest. Until 1949, the Anglo-American occupation powers even sent tens of thousands of arrested refugees back. Only in mid-1952, that is, almost three years after its foundation, did the GDR formally penalize illegal exit when it introduced regulations that allowed the confiscation of the property of citizens who had left East Germany without formal deregistration. And only in September 1954, did *Republikflucht* – absconding from the republic – as well as rendering assistance to illegal border crossing become a crime punishable with prison of up to three years.[100]

On August 20, 1947, the Soviet Military Administration issued its instructions to the East German border police. Article 20b stated that the police was permitted to use firearms in case of the "escape of a violator of the demarcation line, when there are no other means of arrest available (as, f.e., a call to stop, a warning shot in the air)." This permission did *not explicitly* but only *implicitly* stipulate a shoot-to-kill order.[101] The first recorded death of an illegal border crosser shot by East German border police dates to May 7, 1948. But NKVD border guards had killed border crossers as early as August 17, 1945. Incomplete and imprecise record keeping, however, does not allow a precise accounting of the number of deaths at the zonal border between the two emerging German states before the fall of 1949. From the foundation of the GDR on October 7, 1949, to the start of the East German fortification of its border to West Germany in late May 1952, archival records provide evidence

---

[99] Heidemeyer, *Flucht und Zuwanderung aus der SBZ/DDR 1945/1949–1961* (Droste, 1994), pp. 41–46; Dietrich, "Grenzpolizei," p. 207; Manfred Gehrmann, *Die Überwindung des "Eisernen Vorhangs"* (Ch. Links, 2009), p. 56; Keith R. Allen, *Befragung, Überprüfung, Kontrolle* (Ch. Links, 2013), pp. 27.

[100] Kubina, *Ulbrichts Scheitern*, p. 53; Article 8 in "Paß-Gesetz der Deutschen Demokratischen Republik," 9/15/1954, *Gesetzblatt der Deutschen Demokratischen Republik*, 1954/81 (9/22/1954), p. 786.

[101] "Dienstanweisung," 8/20/1947, *Bundesarchiv Lichterfelde*, DO 1/25621, p. 3.

for at least forty-seven killings by East German border police; eleven border guards died in shooting accidents or by suicide.[102]

On May 26, 1952, East German authorities decided to erect obstacles at the 1,393 kilometers of its borders with West Germany and at the 112 kilometers of its zonal borders to West Berlin – but not at the 43 kilometers of its sectoral borders to West Berlin. This policy de facto terminated all local border traffic except in the capital. On June 1, the GDR explicitly permitted the use of firearms to stop refugees at the borders to the Federal Republic. The greater economic incorporation of West Germany into the Western world as well as its planned accession to a yet-to-be-established European Defense Community (EDC) within the North Atlantic Treaty Organization (NATO) merely served East Germany with the pretext to introduce a stricter border regime that had been planned anyways. The strengthening of East Germany's western border, including the incorporation of the border police into the Soviet-style Ministry of State Security, occurred on Stalin's order from March 1952 and in close collaboration with Soviet Control Commission in East Germany.[103]

Initially, the fortifications at the East German border to West Germany consisted of a barbed wire fence at the boundary line, a 10-meter-wide plowed control strip, a 500-meter wide cleared and restricted access border zone with wooden watchtowers and earthen bunkers, and a 5-kilometer restricted area. Hence, the zonal border between the two Germanys started to resemble the Hungarian and Czechoslovak western borders, but lacked the minefields and 5,000-volt electrical fences. The primary goal of this securitized border zone was to force all border crossers to use designated control points, which only interzonal passport holders were allowed to pass. In a forced removal campaign – cynically called operation "Vermin" – the communist government expelled almost 8,400 persons whom it deemed politically unreliable from the 5-kilometer restricted area. Another 6,400 persons avoided removal through escape across the border to West Germany. Still, the vast majority of the population in the restricted area – circa 400,000 residents – were allowed to stay, but was subject to a strict special passport regime. In the three years to May 1955, another twenty-two persons were killed trying to exit illegally across the newly securitized border.[104]

---

[102] Gerhard Schätzlein, "Blutige Grenze 1945 bis 1949," Sälter, *Die vergessenen Toten*, pp. 11–124; Schroeder/Staadt, *Die Todesopfer*, pp. 31–91, 652–57.

[103] Rottman/Taylor, *Berlin Wall*, p. 29; Dietrich, "Grenzpolizei," p. 209; Führ, *Berliner Mauer*, pp. 34–38; Inge Bennewitz, and Rainer Potratz, *Zwangsaussiedlungen an der innerdeutschen Grenze* (Ch. Links, 1994), pp. 26–36.

[104] Volker Ackermann, *Der "echte" Flüchtling* (Universitäts-Verlag Rasch, 1995), pp. 132–33; Horst Gundlach, *Die Grenzüberwachung der DDR* (Rockstuhl, 2014), pp. 7–20; Bennewitz/Potratz, *Zwangsaussiedlungen*, pp. 36–65; Führ, *Berliner Mauer*, pp. 39–40; Schroeder/Staadt, *Die Todesopfer*, pp. 91–118. Among the border guards, only two died by suicide, see p. 654.

The closing of the German–German border by mid-1952 left the German capital as the main escape hatch for East German citizens who wanted to exit. West Berlin's sectoral border to East Berlin and its zonal border to East Germany had been locations of repeated attempts by the GDR regime to discourage escapes since the Soviet blockade in 1948–49. While East Germany could not entirely limit access to West Berlin from East Berlin, it imposed a police ring around all of Berlin to monitor the movement of GDR citizens to the capital. Within Berlin, it closed 200 of the 277 roads that crossed from East to West. After May 1952, the communist regime in the GDR even requested permission from the USSR to close East Berlin's sectoral border to West Berlin completely, but received a negative answer in early 1953. However, in July of 1961, as we will see in Section 8, the Soviet government eventually agreed to the request in order to terminate a steady refugee stream that had gravely destabilized the country's economy and society.[105]

Despite the administrative and political division of Berlin in late 1948 during the Soviet blockade, the city continued to function more or less as one infrastructural unit until August 13, 1961. Berlin's integrated *S-Bahn* (suburban train system) and *U-Bahn* (subway system) allowed moving between the two halves of the city, although East German railroad police checked passengers intermittently. The shoot-to-kill order that had been introduced at the borders to the Federal Republic in June 1952 soon was extended to the zonal borders to West Berlin as well. Still, the refugee stream to the western half of the capital picked up significantly. In the 13 months to June 1953 alone, 189,530 refugees were registered officially as new arrivals there. Eventually 96 percent of all recognized refugees were flown out to West Germany, with the rest being settled in West Berlin. The loss of labor to the East German economy was so significant that the regime launched a policy to convince and even force East Germans and East Berliners holding regular jobs in West Berlin to take up work in the GDR. Still, twenty-five persons were killed by border police between January 1949 and May 1955, despite the relative openness of the sectoral borders that allowed hundreds of thousands of Berliners to cross daily the urban line of division for work, shopping, leisure, and personal visits to friends and family.[106]

---

[105] Führ, *Berliner Mauer*, p. 7; Dietrich, "Grenzpolizei," p. 209; Dietmar Schultke, *Keiner kommt durch* (Aufbau, 2017), p. 37; Jan Foitzik, Werner Künzel, Anette Leo, and Martina Weyrauch, eds., *Das Jahr 1953* (Brandenburgische Landeszentrale für politische Bildung, 2003, 2004), p. 48; Kubina, *Ulbrichts Scheitern*, pp. 39–53, 98–103.

[106] Udo Dittfurth, *August 1961* (Gesellschaft für Eisenbahngeschichte und Eisenbahnwesen, 2003), pp. 16–25; "[Monthly table for January 1952 to August 1960]," [September? 1960], *Landesarchiv Berlin*, B Rep. 077, Nr. 651, p. 1; Heidemeyer, *Flucht*, pp. 139–44; Frank Roggenbuch, *Das Berliner Grenzgängerproblem* (De Gruyter, 2008); Sälter, *Die vergessenen Toten*, pp. 97–191.

After Stalin's death in early March 1953, his successors tried to convince the East German leadership to undo some of the extreme economic policies that were co-responsible for the continued refugee stream to West Berlin. However, once the communist government announced the reversal of some of them on June 9, it provoked the well-known uprising that almost toppled the communist regime a week later. Soviet occupation troops eventually suppressed demonstrations and strikes. In the immediate wake of the uprising, the East German regime and the Soviet army officially closed access to West Berlin for local residents for a week. Still, East Germans and East Berliners – including residents working in the other half of the city and strikers who tried to escape the post-uprising crackdown – were creative in circumventing the closed borders by slipping through backyards and swimming through waterways. The East German regime managed to blame the original Soviet proposals to relax the economic situation for the outbreak of the uprising, and hence doubled down in pursuing the very policies that had primarily caused the swelling refugee stream. Between June 1953 and May 1955, another 377,567 persons fled to West Berlin.[107]

The year 1955 marked a major turning point in the history of the Iron Curtain in Europe, as the next two sections show. Despite the suppression of the East German uprising in June 1953, the post-Stalinist leadership pursued a policy of relaxation of tensions with the West in the following two years. Its most important result was the agreement to end the joint Allied occupation of Austria, but this unfortunately did not extend to Germany. France's failure to ratify the EDC in August 1954 initially pleased the USSR, but simultaneously raised the issue of direct NATO membership of West Germany. Eventually, the Anglo-American-French Allies decided to award almost complete sovereignty to the Federal Republic on May 5, 1955, and allow West Germany to accede to NATO the following day. The USSR reacted with the ad hoc foundation of the Warsaw Pact on May 14, 1955, largely in the vain hope of creating a bargaining chip that would lead to the simultaneous dissolution of both alliance systems. This all happened, however, immediately before the signing of the Austrian State Treaty on May 15 that ended Allied occupation there by October. In September, the USSR also awarded the GDR partial sovereignty, which meant that the East German regime was allowed to guard its external borders by itself, but was not allowed to control Western Allied access to West Berlin.[108] While by late 1955,

---

[107] Kubina, *Ulbrichts Scheitern*, pp. 103–21; Kowalczuk, *17. Juni 1953*, p. 51; Jens Schöne, *Volksaufstand* (Berlin Story Verlag, 2013), p. 7; Gehrmann, *Überwindung*, pp, 76–78; "[Monthly table for January 1952 to August 1960]," [September? 1960], *Landesarchiv Berlin*, B Rep. 077, Nr. 651, p. 1.

[108] Rolf Steininger, *Der Staatsvertrag* (Studien Verlag, 2005), pp. 127–50; Lüthi, *Cold Wars*, pp. 31–32; "Vertrag," [9/20/1955], *Bundesarchiv Lichterfelde*, NY 4090/471, pp. 205–207; Führ, *Berliner Mauer*, p. 46.

Map 9 Swiss newspaper map of the Iron Curtain in the late 1950s.
Source: *Die Tat*, October 2, 1959, p. 39.

Germany emerged physically and legally divided, Berlin still functioned as one urban unit.

On April 5, 1955, Churchill had resigned from the second of his two terms as British prime minister. Nine years and one month after his famous speech in Fulton, Missouri, his iconic Iron Curtain metaphor had become reality on the ground (Map 9). From Lübeck in the Baltic to Burgas at the Black Sea, an Iron Curtain had descended across the continent. Behind that fortified and partially mined line lay all the capitals of the ancient states of Central and Eastern Europe: Warsaw, Berlin, Prague, Budapest, Belgrade, Bucharest, and Sofia. Newspaper maps from the time showed a thick line running through Europe. At the northern end, the border was somewhat further west than Churchill had predicted in 1946; at the southern, it was much further east. And Albania emerged as a ringed quasi-island sandwiched between neutral Yugoslavia, NATO member Greece, and the Adriatic.[109]

---
[109] *NSJ*, 2/18/1955:1; *HS*, 5/17/1955:42.

7 Czechoslovakia's and Hungary's Divergent Border Regimes, 1955–1989

With West German accession to NATO on May 6, 1955, and the conclusion of the Austrian State Treaty nine days later, Czechoslovakia faced a Cold War enemy across its western border while Hungary suddenly shared a boundary with a neutral neighbor. These different geopolitical realities as well as dissimilar subsequent political developments between the two countries resulted in diverging evolutions of their border regimes until 1989. In the late 1950s, both countries simultaneously softened their rigid passport and border regimes, largely for economic reasons. However, since the Soviet suppression of the Hungarian Revolution had happened in 1956, Hungary's opening continued unimpeded over the course of the remaining three decades of the Cold War. In comparison, the USSR intervened in the CSSR in 1968, cutting short the opening and hence ensuring the return to the previous rigid system. Unsurprisingly, Czechoslovakia's Iron Curtain was the last to disappear in Central Europe; it tumbled in early December of 1989 – three decades after Yugoslavia's, seven months after Hungary's, and six weeks after East Germany's.

Czechoslovakia reacted to West German NATO accession in May 1955 with an overhaul of its border fortifications, particularly the 5,000-volt electrical fences, which were designed to keep its own citizens in but not to keep Western armies out. Authorities also destroyed buildings in empty villages – particularly in those from which the *Sudetendeutsche* had been expelled in 1945–46 – within a 15-kilometer-wide border area. The introduction of mandatory military training for all male citizens between 16 and 26 served the creation of a pool of manpower from which future border guards could be conscripted. The sudden Czechoslovak removal of minefields in the summer of 1956 seemed to respond to the official Soviet launch of de-Stalinization the previous February, but in reality occurred largely due to the increased number of incidental explosions – including the killings of border guards – by poorly manufactured mines. The removal led to an increase of escapes but also to a rise of lethal incidents at the Czechoslovak–Austrian border in the summer of 1956 that further undermined bilateral relations. Yet, the communist regime concurrently reviewed its strict passport policy in place since 1945. Starting on July 1, 1956, citizens were allowed to apply to undertake private trips to fraternal socialist countries.[110]

The withdrawal of Soviet troops from Austria in October of 1955 did not precipitate a similar Soviet retreat from occupation in Hungary. Earlier that year,

---

[110] Meinke, "Zweimal," p. 57; Meinke, *Entwicklung*, pp. 30–32; NZZ-e, 6/20/1955:2; NZZ-e, 8/9/1945:2; Rychlík, *Cestování do ciziny*, p. 55.

the communist regime in Budapest had just completed a multiyear overhaul of its fortifications at the Yugoslav and Austrian border. Yet, even before the conclusion of the Austrian State Treaty on May 15, the Hungarian government had called for a reestablishment of good neighborly relations, which eventually led to a softening of the Hungarian exit and entry rules as well as the establishment of diplomatic relations by the fall. After mid-1955, Hungary anteceded Czechoslovakia in removing mines from the border, mainly for the same reasons. And in November, the removal of all physical obstacles at the border to Yugoslavia started. Three months after the official Soviet launch of de-Stalinization in February 1956, the Hungarian government also decided on a similar removal at the border to Austria – just less than a year after it had completed its border regime overhaul.[111]

The political developments that eventually led to the Hungarian Revolution on October 23, 1956, had an impact on the country's border as well. The removal of border fortifications to Austria in the five months beforehand increased the monthly number of escapees without proper documents from 200 to 1,000. Yet, trains running between Vienna and Budapest carried for the first time customs officials checking Hungarian and foreign passport and visa holders en route; as a result, time-consuming stops at the border disappeared. On October 21, the barriers at Felsőcsatár/Burg even opened for the local Austrian population to visit a Hungarian wine festival without passports or visas. Once the revolution started two days later, however, the border shut again. But within days, it de facto reopened, as Hungarian guards were withdrawn to help in the initial suppression of the revolution or left on their own volition to support it. By late October, local populations from both sides of the entire border reconnected with each other in mutual visits. Simultaneously, hundreds of refugees escaping from armed conflict in Budapest and other Hungarian cities crossed the now unguarded border every day.[112]

The Soviet military intervention in Hungary on November 4 shocked local populations on both sides. Around 10,000 refugees crossed the border on that day alone. Until the year's end, 163,000 Hungarians fled to Austria, with tens of thousands more to the summer of 1957. Reportedly, 70,000 escaped across a

---

[111] István Balló, "Zur militärischen Geschichte Ungarns nach dem Zweiten Weltkrieg," Heeresgeschichtliches Museum Wien, *Eiserne Vorhang*, p. 77; Szorger/Bayer, *Burgenland*, pp. 7–8; Lajos Gecsényi, "Die Beziehungen zwischen Ungarn und Österreich 1954–1964," Heeresgeschichtliches Museum Wien, *Eiserne Vorhang*, pp. 56–61; József Lugosi, "Keine Grenze wie jede andere," Heeresgeschichtliches Museum Wien, *Eiserne Vorhang*, p. 85; Varga, "Technische und mentalitätsgeschichtliche Aspekte," p. 120; *NZZ*-n, 10/10/1955:2; *WP*, 12/15/1955:4.

[112] Varga, "Technische und mentalitätsgeschichtliche Aspekte," pp. 120–22; Bencsik/Nagy, *A magyar úti okmányok története*, p. 27; *Tat*, 10/23/1956:12; *NZZ*-m, 10/26/1956:2; Gáspár, "A második," p. 44; *NZZ*-e, 10/31/1945:5.

small wooden canal bridge near Andau, until a Soviet tank shell destroyed it on November 21. Later that month, Soviet and Hungarian border guards started to block systematically the stream of refugees.[113]

In early January of 1957, the new, post-revolutionary and pro-Soviet Hungarian government decided to rebuild the border fortifications to Austria and Yugoslavia, which its reformist predecessor had removed between November 1955 and mid-1956. The following month, restricted zones at the borders to both countries reappeared. Escape attempts, including assistance, were put under punishment with up to five years in prison. From April to June, the Hungarian army fortified various stretches along the border to Austria with a double barbed wire fence, the laying of 800,000 mines, or both. Border units guarded the boundary line aggressively, shooting at photographers on Austrian territory or pursuing escapees there. In mid-1957, Hungary even reimposed the shoot-to-kill order. A year later, the last gap in Hungary's reestablished Iron Curtain to Austria closed when Hungary erected a fence running along the borderline through the shallow *Neusiedler See*.[114]

Of course, refugees still attempted to cross in the following years, even as numbers drastically declined. Escapees pole-vaulted across the 2.5-meter-high fence, crawled through the flood-lighted border zone, or laid planks over barbed wire fences. Many were killed, gravely hurt, or maimed when they stepped on mines; some lost limbs in emergency surgeries in Austrian hospitals. Mines dislodged in rainstorms still killed Hungarian service men and injured Austrian farmers in nearby vineyards. Hungarian border guards recurrently engaged in gun battles with local police on Austrian territory. Yet, due to their intimate knowledge of the border, they, too, continued to escape.[115]

In the late 1950s, Czechoslovakia started to open its borders for Western tourists because it urgently needed to augment its hard currency reserves. In 1963, the country even reopened all border crossing points to Austria and West Germany which it had closed a decade before. Since Austria insisted on reciprocity in cross-border travel, the CSSR was forced to allow tourist groups to travel to its capitalist neighbor, but limited currency reserves still kept their number low. Initially, the government used a political selection process to reward citizens for political reliability. And yet, some of those selected still

---

[113] Varga, "Technische und mentalitätsgeschichtliche Aspekte," p. 123; Sarah Knoll, "Flucht über den 'Eisernen Vorhang'," *Storia e Regione*, 30/2 (2021), pp. 44–49; Gáspár, "A második," p. 46; *GM*, 11/22/1956:45; *AS*, 11/21/1956:1; *DBG*, 11/21/1956:1.

[114] Gecsényi, "Beziehungen," pp. 64, 67; *NZZ*-m, 2/9/1957:5; Lugosi, "Keine Grenze," p. 86; *LAT*, 4/7/1957:3; *NZN*, 4/10/1957:5; Gáspár, "A második," p. 46; *CDT*, 7/25/1958:4.

[115] Szorger/Bayer, *Burgenland*, p. 10; *WP*, 8/2/1958:2; *HC*, 11/18/1959:15b; *CDT*, 12/10/1959:A4; *SCMP*, 5/7/1957:16; *NZZ*-m, 3/5/1960:2; *Tat*, 9/21/1960:9; *NZZ*-m, 5/8/1957:5; *NZZ*-m, 4/20/1960:2; *Bund*-m, 11/29/1960:8; *WP*, 7/25/1961:A23.

defected once they had arrived in Vienna. But by 1963, the Czechoslovak regime decided to regard foreign travel no longer as a reward but an ordinary matter open to all citizens. While travel to fraternal socialist states in East Europe became normalized throughout the 1960s, trips to Yugoslavia with its relatively open borders to the West (see Section 3) and to Austria still remained sensitive for political and financial reasons. Unauthorized exit and refusal to return could be punished with prison up to five years. But since this legal statute was unenforceable once offenders had left the country permanently, the CSSR changed the punishment from prison to confiscation of property. Only a few citizens, particularly the remaining *Sudetendeutsche*, were allowed to emigrate legally.[116]

Despite this gradual liberalization, the Czechoslovak border regime remained as brutal as it had been before, even if it removed the 5,000-volt electrical fence in 1966. Earlier in the decade, the border fortifications had undergone yet another modernization. Czechoslovak border guards still recurrently violated West German and Austrian sovereignty in pursuit of escapees. Nevertheless, Czechoslovak, Polish, and East German citizens succeeded in swimming through border rivers, crossing the fortified border by foot or in armored vehicles, being smuggled out in cars of western visitors, or flying across in planes. Even border guards decided to abscond; two managed to crash an army truck through the barriers, for example.[117]

Over the course of the 1960s, the continued violence at the Czechoslovak border developed into a sensitive issue in Austrian politics. An incident of indiscriminate shooting at refugees even after they had reached Austrian territory in mid-August 1967 eventually soured Austrian–Czechoslovak governmental relations. Despite a quick official apology by the communist government, its border units repeated the practice within two weeks, this time killing an East German citizen on Austrian territory. The government in Vienna protested once more, but this time its counterpart in Prague decided not to apologize but to launch an ideological smear campaign in its media, unnecessarily deepening the diplomatic crisis.[118]

In parallel to Czechoslovakia, Hungary, too, opened up its borders to Western tourists in the late 1950s. In 1961, the revision of the 1948 passport law allowed Hungarian citizens to travel into the other direction as well, as long as they were

---

[116] Perzi, "Leben," p. 113; *NZZ*-m, 12/5/1963:1; Rychlík, *Cestování do ciziny*, pp. 57–79; *BT*, 6/17/1958:8; *NZN*, 1/6/1964:12; *NZZ*-e, 4/2/1964:2; *NZZ*-m, 11/14/1964:2.
[117] Meinke, "Zweimal," p. 58; Meinke, *Entwicklung*, pp. 34–35; *Bund*, 8/5/1958:1; *NZZ*-e, 10/20/1958:2; *AA*, 6/17/1962:B1; *Bund*-m, 4/28/1964:8; *Bund*-n, 9/7/1964:16; *HC*, 8/28/1958:21a; *HC*, 9/7/1958:15A; *AA*, 6/17/1962:B1; *CDT*, 11/27/1959:21; *Guardian*, 8/16/1961:7; *HC*, 4/14/1965:28; *Tat*, 11/18/1958:2; *CT*, 10/8/1963:4.
[118] *Bund*, 8/18/1967:2; *NZZ*-m, 8/22/1967:1; *HC*, 8/28/1967:16a; *NZN*, 9/8/1967:1.

not carriers of state secrets. This allowed Hungarian citizens to visit relatives who had fled in 1956–57, but barred private travel by party members. Within two years, Hungary issued over 200,000 passports and exit visas in an unbureaucratic fashion. Unsurprisingly, thousands decided not to return from visits to the West but to stay with escaped family members and start a new life abroad. Within a couple of years, this "brain drain" worried the communist regime in Hungary, but Budapest decided neither to make the continued outflow into a political issue nor reverse its liberalized passport policies. Unlike Czechoslovakia, Hungary even tried to reestablish local cross-border traffic on special occasions, as, for example, during the summer theater festival in Sopron in 1963, which Austrians could visit without passports. Yet, the barbed wire fences and the mines at the border remained in place, posing a continued danger to escapees, border guards, and Austrian farmers.[119]

All the same, over the entire period of the 1960s, the Hungarian communist government rethought its border regime. The lethal border strip had created reputational costs that undermined its attempts to welcome foreign tourists and businesses. As early as 1960, the restricted border area was narrowed from 15 to 5–8 kilometers. Simultaneously, the problematic mines were removed at some border stretches in a controlled detonation campaign, although over one million new mines were laid until 1963 while the barbed wire fences were reinforced with concrete pillars. Yet, in the summer of 1961, Hungarian and Austrian officials met at the border to discuss the exact positions of border markers. The visit of Austria's foreign minister to Budapest in late 1964 clearly dealt with the issue; before his departure, he expressed the hope that the mine-and-barbed wire-free state at the Austrian–Yugoslav border would become a reality at the Austrian–Hungarian border as well. Still, in mid-1965, a dislodged mine that gravely injured an Austrian boy led to a major diplomatic blowup between the two governments. In the same year, Hungarian machine guns sprayed a bus that crashed through the border with bullets, and border guards continued to violate Austrian sovereignty in pursuit of escapees.[120]

Nevertheless, on May 11, 1965, the Hungarian communist regime decided to remove all mines from the border to Austria; the multiyear removal itself started in September. But since the shoot-to-kill order remained in place, serious border

---

[119] Bencsik/Nagy, *A magyar úti okmányok története*, pp. 56–60; *CT*, 8/11/1963:A1; *JP*, 12/1/1963:3; *WP*, 6/25/1963:A20; *NZZ*-e, 4/13/1960:5.

[120] Andreas Schmidt-Schweizer, "Motive im Vorfeld der Demontage des 'Eisernen Vorhangs', 1987–1989," Peter Haslinger, ed., *Grenze im Kopf* (Peter Lang, 1999), p. 128; Bencsik/Nagy, *A magyar úti okmányok története*, p. 48; *SCMP*, 4/14/1960:12; Lugosi, "Keine Grenze," p. 89; Gecsényi, "Beziehungen," p. 73; *NZN*, 10/29/1964:6; Maximilain Graf, "Ein Musterbeispiel der europäischen Entspannung?" Szabó, *Österreich*, p. 262; *Bund*-n, 6/22/1965:14; *Tat*, 9/6/1965:2.

incidents continued into the second half of the 1960s. By 1969, however, the border appeared in a transformed state. Since 1965, the Hungarian government had tested a Soviet electronic surveillance system with alarm wires at some border stretches; its effectiveness in detecting ongoing escape attempts allowed not only the complete removal of minefields and other obstacles – except for a simple barbed wire fence at the border line – but also the abolition of the restricted border zone. The new system prevented 92–95 percent of the 400–1,000 annual escape attempts between 1970 and 1988. Nevertheless, nine border crossers were shot dead in this period.[121]

Czechoslovakia's border regime moved into the opposite direction by the end of the 1960s. The Soviet-led Warsaw Pact military intervention on August 21, 1968, terminated the short-lived Prague Spring. Over the spring and summer, the reform government had studied a complete overhaul of its passport system, including the abolition of exit visas for travel to the West. Yet, the Soviet-led intervention triggered a one-year-long reversal of the nascent opening of the country. As early as August 26, the USSR forced the CSSR to commit to the reconstruction of its passport and border regime. For around two months, Soviet troops staffed the border to Austria and West Germany. Czechoslovakia also closed all border crossing points – except one – to Austria for a decade, while it increased those to West Germany from three to four in a political show by mid-1969. Possibly, the advent of *Ostpolitik* in the Federal Republic, including its attempts to find a modus vivendi with the USSR, Poland, the CSSR, and the GDR, played a role in this differentiated border policy.[122]

Interestingly, the Czechoslovak government continued to issue passports and exit visas for some time after the August 21 intervention. Under Soviet pressure the CSSR eventually tightened the possibilities for its citizens to travel to the West by November, and curbed them widely, but not completely, within another thirteen months. The quick closing of the borders in late August also prevented an exodus similar to the one from Hungary after October 1956. Still, over 4,000 citizens managed to leave illegally – sometimes with the connivance of sympathetic Czechoslovak border guards – while many more decided not to return from their visits abroad.[123]

The tightened border regime after August 21, 1968, again led to numerous incidents. A GDR citizen escaped in late September, but narrowly avoided

---

[121] Lugosi, "Keine Grenze," pp. 90–92; *BT*, 9/24/1965:12; *NZN*, 7/3/1967:2; *Bund*, 5/16/1968:36; *NZZ*-m, 5/24/1968:9; Gáspár, "A második," p. 47; Szorger/Bayer, *Burgenland*, pp. 10–11; Schmidt-Schweizer, "Motive," p. 129–30.
[122] Rychlík, *Cestování do ciziny*, pp. 79–80; *NYT*, 6/13/1968:7; Meinke, *Entwicklung*, pp. 43–44; *Bund*, 8/28/1968:32; *BG*, 8/29/1968:18; *NYT*, 10/26/1968:8; Perzi, "Leben," p. 115; Lüthi, *Cold Wars*, pp. 429–39.
[123] Perzi, "Leben," pp. 114–15; Rychlík, *Cestování do ciziny*, pp. 82–87, 90, 110–122.

arrest by Czechoslovak border guards on Austrian territory by screaming loudly for help. In January, border guards again caught up with two fleeing East German citizens 600 meters into West German territory and returned with them to Czechoslovakia. A truck failed crashing through the same border in a hail of Czechoslovak bullets in July; one person was killed and the others arrested. Repeated West German and Austrian diplomatic protests against the pursuit of escapees outside of Czechoslovak territory did not change this practice. The deterioration of bilateral relations eventually convinced the CSSR to agree to a joint commission with Austria to investigate border incidents in 1973.[124] Still, the relationship did not improve, despite the simultaneous political normalization process between Czechoslovakia and West Germany. And Prague continued to modernize its border fortifications. Even the Czechoslovak signing of the Helsinki Final Act on August 1, 1975, which called for an increase of East–West contacts, did not soften the communist government's rigid stance. Unsurprisingly, the CSSR was the object of repeated international criticism for its non-compliance with the Final Act at the triannual Helsinki follow-up meetings. Throughout the 1980s, lethal border incidents continued to burden Czechoslovakia's governmental relations with both Austria and West Germany.[125]

In comparison, the creation of a relatively non-lethal, though still effective, border regime at the Hungarian–Austrian border in 1969 set Budapest on the road to a further opening over the course of the 1970s. Initially, exit visas were still required for travel to the non-socialist world, which was one reason incidents continued to happen. In mid-April 1970, for example, a Hungarian citizen without an exit visa hijacked a bus en route from Budapest to Vienna and threatened to kill all passengers with a bomb if he was not allowed to pass the border. After hours of negotiations, the hijacker allowed all passengers to disembark, but was shot dead by Hungarian border guards when he tried to re-kidnap some of them outside of the bus.[126] Yet, the Helsinki Final Act had a major impact on Hungary's passport and border policies. Unlike Prague, Budapest was more inclined to fulfill its commitments, particularly under Vienna's economic pressure. In May 1978, Hungary and Austria agreed to abolish visa requirements for visits by each other's citizens; the new rule went into effect on January 1, 1979. In the decade to September 1989, the Hungarian border guard service only enforced its government's agreements with other

---

[124] *Bund*, 9/25/1968:26; *NZN*, 1/6/1969:9; *Tat*, 7/15/1969:2; *BT*, 1/14/1971:1; *Bund*, 5/21/1972:4; *NZZ*, 5/11/1972:2; *NZN*, 5/15/1972:2; *Bund*, 3/5/1973:1.

[125] *NZN*, 12/14/1973:1; *Guardian*, 8/4/1973:11; Rychlík, *Cestování do ciziny*, pp. 93–95; *NZZ*, 11/7/1984:4; *Bund*, 11/4/1984:3; *WP*, 11/25/1984:28; *NZZ*, 3/2/1985:4; *NZN*, 9/22/1986:8.

[126] Bencsik/Nagy, *A magyar úti okmányok története*, p. 72; *NZN*, 4/16/1970:2.

socialist states to prevent escapes of their citizens to the West, as, for example, Soviets, East Germans, Romanians, or Poles.[127]

In 1989, the opening of the Iron Curtain at the Hungarian and Czechoslovak borders to the Western world occurred in the context of Soviet reform policies since 1985 and the collapse of the communist government in East Germany, as described in the next section. Hungary started to remove its rusty barbed wire fence in early May 1989. The country's foreign minister met with his Austrian counterpart on June 27, 1989, to cut symbolically the Iron Curtain with giant wire cutters. However, Hungary's border guards continued to prevent illegal border crossing attempts by citizens of other socialist states, particularly East German tourists, throughout July and August. Some of those arrested were expelled to the GDR. Yet, tens of thousands of East German tourists refused to return home and hoped for another chance to escape via Austria to the Federal Republic. By August, mass escape attempts had become daily and particularly nightly occurrences. Tragically, the very last person to die at the Iron Curtain that cut through Central Europe was an East German citizen, who was hit on August 21 by a bullet accidentally fired from a Hungarian border guard gun during a scuffle on the boundary line itself. After negotiations with the West German government, Hungary opened its borders on September 11 to allow tens of thousands of GDR citizens to leave via Austria. It thereby broke its agreements with other socialist states to prevent the exit of their citizens.[128] The Iron Curtain at the Austrian–Hungarian border was gone.

Czechoslovakia appeared almost untouched by the events in Hungary in August and September. At that very time, thousands of East German tourists occupied the West German embassy in Prague in the hope of receiving permission to emigrate to the Federal Republic, but not a single Czechoslovak citizen joined them. The communist regime continued to suppress any show of domestic dissent, until its police beat up student protesters, who had convened in Prague on November 17 to observe the fiftieth anniversary of the killing of a student by German Nazis. It was the death knell to the regime, as mass popular protest erupted within days. Within a week of the start of roundtable discussions on November 27 on the formation of a coalition government between dissidents and communists, the interior ministry simply cancelled all travel prohibitions. On December 17, the new Czechoslovak foreign minister, a protagonist of the

---

[127] Bencsik/Nagy, *A magyar úti okmányok története*, p. 75; *GM*, 5/6/1978:15; *CSM*, 1/4/1979:5; Gáspár, "A második," p. 48; *SCMP*, 8/11/1983:18; *NZN*, 5/17/1982:8; Schmidt-Schweizer, "Motive," p. 134.

[128] Technical Museum Brno, *Eiserne Vorhang*, pp. 147–49; Szorger/Bayer, *Burgenland*, p. 13–16; Gáspár, "A második," p. 48; Tamás Baranyi, Maximilian Graf, Melinda Krajczar, and Isabella Lehner, "A Masterpiece of European Détente? Austrian–Hungarian Relations from 1964 until the Peaceful End of the Cold War," *Zeitgeschichte*, 41/5 (2014), pp. 324–26.

Prague Spring, met his Austrian colleague to cut the Iron Curtain with giant wire cutters at the joint border, repeating the publicity stunt at the Hungarian border from half a year before.[129] It was the last Iron Curtain in Central Europe to tumble. As described in the next section, the Iron Curtains dividing Berlin and Germany had already started to disappear on November 9.

8 East Germany's Walls

In comparison to the fortified borders of Yugoslavia, Hungary, and Czechoslovakia, the walls that divided Berlin and Germany after 1961 were the most extreme cases of Iron Curtains. They emerged at a time when Yugoslavia was relaxing its border regime and Hungary was disarming its western border, as described in previous sections. The primary purpose of the East German border fortifications after August 13, 1961, was to stabilize the country's faltering economy, which had failed to catch up with its capitalist sibling in West Germany. Instead of seeking economic reform that would make socialism palatable to its citizens, the GDR spent its stretched state budget to fortify its borders with walls and minefields to prevent its population from escaping. The communist regime still collapsed in late 1989 after tens of thousands of its citizens had fled via an opening Hungary.

Due to competing statistics that use different methodologies of counting and include estimates of refugees who never officially registered, the number of East German citizens leaving for West Berlin and West Germany during the entire 1945–61 period remains uncertain, but probably amounts to at least 2.75 million. The continued flight took a toll on East Germany's society and economy. Between 1950 and 1961, East Germany's population shrank by 1.309 million from 18.388 million to 17.079 million, taking into account immigration, live births, and deaths. Since the majority of refugees were young and disproportionally well-educated adults in working age, their sudden and often unannounced exit threatened the economic future of East German socialism.[130]

Even East Germany's assumption of partial sovereignty in the fall of 1955 did not affect the stream of refugees to West Berlin and West Germany. After May 1955, the month of the Federal Republic's accession to NATO, the GDR completed setting up barbed wire fences at its entire western border, followed by the introduction of a double barbed wire fence in 1958. These were not defensive fortifications but obstacles to prevent illegal exit. But escapes across that long and only tentatively secured border continued in the hundreds of

---

[129] Frederick Taylor, *The Berlin Wall* (HarperCollins, 2006), pp. 404–6; Lüthi, *Cold Wars*, pp. 588–89; Rychlík, *Cestování do ciziny*, p. 132.

[130] Heidemeyer, *Flucht*, pp. 47, 51; for demographic developments, see: www.statista.com/statistics/1054199/population-of-east-and-west-germany/, accessed on January 24, 2025.

thousands. In comparison to the situation at the German–German border, the German capital still functioned as a single urban unit, although the GDR progressively tried to control access to West Berlin as well. From June 1955 to the closing of the borders around West Berlin on August 13, 1961, almost 900,000 arriving refugees were officially registered in the western half of capital. In the same period, around 1.36 million refugees were officially registered in West Germany – a number, however, that includes a non-quantifiable majority of the 900,000 refugees registered as arrivals in West Berlin. In the six years to mid-August 1961, twenty-nine border crossers died at the German–German border and nine in Berlin.[131]

Berlin also served as an escape hatch for citizens from the USSR and East Europe. Members of the Soviet occupation forces frequently defected to West Berlin. A conductor of the Prague National Theater Opera fled in May of 1956 while on tour in East Berlin. Members of the Hungarian trade mission absconded after the Soviet suppression of the revolution the following November. A sacked Polish vice-minister slipped into West Berlin in the late summer of 1957. But even ordinary citizens without travel permits managed to flee. In 1953, three Czechoslovak men arrived after a 28-day hiking journey that had led them through the cleared, guarded, and fortified Czechoslovak border area, East Germany by night, and then gunfire at the East Berlin border to West Berlin. In 1959, two Poles escaped in a freight train on a 9-day long ride without sufficient food and water.[132] Unsurprisingly, the Czechoslovak and Polish governments started to guard their borders to the GDR to prevent escapes by their citizens to West Berlin, as mentioned in previous sections.

On November 10, 1958, Soviet leader Khrushchev issued his infamous ultimatum, demanding the renegotiation of Western Allied rights in West Berlin within six months while threatening the unilateral transfer of Soviet control of Western access to West Berlin through the GDR. By all accounts, he had not discussed this move with the East German leaders. It is also doubtful that he was serious about his own ultimatum since this would have deprived the USSR of a political tool of actual influence in Germany. In any case, nothing happened when the ultimatum expired in May 1959; Khrushchev even formally withdrew it during his seminal visit to the United States in September. He probably had hoped to use West Berlin as a lever to get concessions on unrelated issues, including his invitation to the White House. However, the East German

---

[131] Monthly statistics in: *Landesarchiv Berlin*, B Rep. 077, Nr. 651 and 652; Meinke, "Zweimal," p. 57; Ackermann, *Der "echte" Flüchtling*, pp. 289–91; Schroeder/Staadt, *Die Todesopfer*, pp. 112–54; Sälter, *Die vergessenen Toten*, pp. 191–223.

[132] *WP*, 12/4/1949:B5; *NYT*, 2/21/1954:4; *CDT*, 7/8/1956:29; *NYT*, 11/8/1956:15; *HC*, 9/8/1957:27A; *NYT*, 11/4/1953:12; *WP*, 5/26/1959:A4.

leader Walter Ulbricht understood the unexpected ultimatum as a means to seize West Berlin and thereby close the escape hatch. A fortnight after Khrushchev's ultimatum, East Germany's communist leaders prohibited the border police from using firearms so as not to endanger any Allied negotiations on West Berlin. However, after the failure of the Allied summit in Paris in May 1960, the GDR reinstated the shoot-to-kill order on June 15. Still, six people died at the German–German border and in Berlin during this period – two were shot, three drowned, and one committed suicide after arrest.[133]

The failure of the Vienna Summit between Khrushchev and US President John F. Kennedy in early June 1961 to come to terms on Germany set the stage for the decision to close the borders around West Berlin. Refugee numbers had steadily increased over the previous year to such a degree that East Germany's economy was close to collapse. In January of 1961, Ulbricht had admitted to Khrushchev that the departure of over two million East German citizens to West Germany had brought his country's underperforming economy close to the breaking point. By then, the East German leader had given up on getting West Berlin; he now aimed at permanently closing the escape hatch by shuttering the borders. Since his ultimate goal was the economic integration of the GDR into the Socialist Camp, Ulbricht started to mobilize economic and political support from the USSR and socialist East Europe in March. Without any feasible alternative in sight, Khrushchev agreed on July 20 to the sealing of East Germany's zonal borders and East Berlin's sectoral borders to West Berlin. Even before the final Soviet approval, the East German communist regime had scheduled the closing of the border for Sunday, August 13, and had started to prepare the necessary material and personnel resources.[134]

In the early hours of August 13, 20,000 members of the East German police, army, and auxiliary units guarded the 43 kilometers of the sectoral border between East and West Berlin. Within hours, barbed wire and in some cases primitive walls sprang up on streets crossing the sectoral border. The S-Bahn and U-Bahn lines linking the two halves of the city either stopped crossing the border or rushed through stations in West Berlin and East Berlin that had no

---

[133] Hope M. Harrison, *Driving the Soviets up the Wall* (Princeton University Press, 2003), pp. 96–138; Matthias Uhl, *Krieg um Berlin?* (Oldenbourg, 2008), pp. 87–113; "Protokoll," 11/26/1958, *Bundesarchiv Freiburg*, DVW 1/39565, p. 3; "Direktive," 6/15/1960, *Bundesarchiv Freiburg*, DVW 1/39459, p. 41; Schroeder/Staadt, *Die Todesopfer*, pp. 112–54; Sälter, *Die vergessenen Toten*, pp. 191–223.

[134] Harrison, *Driving*, pp. 139–223; Monthly statistics in: *Landesarchiv Berlin*, B Rep. 077, Nr. 651 and 652; Taylor, *Berlin Wall*, p. 136; "Teurer Genosse Nikita Sergejewitsch," 1/19/1961, *Bundesarchiv Lichterfelde*, DY 30/3508, pg. 72–73; "Beratungsmaterial," 7/11/1961, *Bundesarchiv Lichterfelde*, DE 4/28087, various pages; "Rede," no date, *Bundesarchiv Lichterfelde*, DY 30/3405, pp. 1–8; Manfred Wilke, "Der Weg zur Mauer," Eckhard Jesse, ed., *Eine Mauer für den SED-Staat* (Duncker & Humblot, 2012), pp. 32–36.

official border crossing points. GDR propaganda claimed that the closing of the border had preserved world peace since it had supposedly preempted an imminent West German military attack. These claims obviously were hyperbolic, but long-standing class warfare rhetoric had convinced a significant portion of the GDR population of the necessity of this step, at least according to the monitoring of public opinion by the secret service.[135]

By December of 1961, the GDR erected sturdier walls, including watchtowers and anti-vehicle obstacles, along parts of the sectoral border to West Berlin (Map 10). Within days after August 13, East Germany also bricked up windows in buildings standing at that boundary line to prevent refugees from jumping into West Berlin. Until early October, the GDR forced over 3,000 East Berlin residents out of their bricked-up buildings. On September 15, a month after the closing of the border around West Berlin, the GDR also transferred the border police to the East German Army, indicating that the securitization of the border was no longer a policing matter but a military issue.[136]

Map 10 In August 1961, East Germany first closed the border between East and West Berlin and then built a wall over the following years.

Source: Berlin, Germany, 1963, Presse- und Informationsamt des Landes Berlin

---

[135] Rottman/Taylor, *Berlin Wall*, p. 32; Dittfurth, *August 1961*; "[Rede von] Genosse Walter Ulbricht (8/20/1961)," *Bundesarchiv Lichterfelde*, DY 30/11771, pp. 95–114; Robert Rauh, *Die Mauer war doch richtig!* (Be.bra, 2021).

[136] Rottman/Taylor, *Berlin Wall*, pp. 32–33, 42, 69.

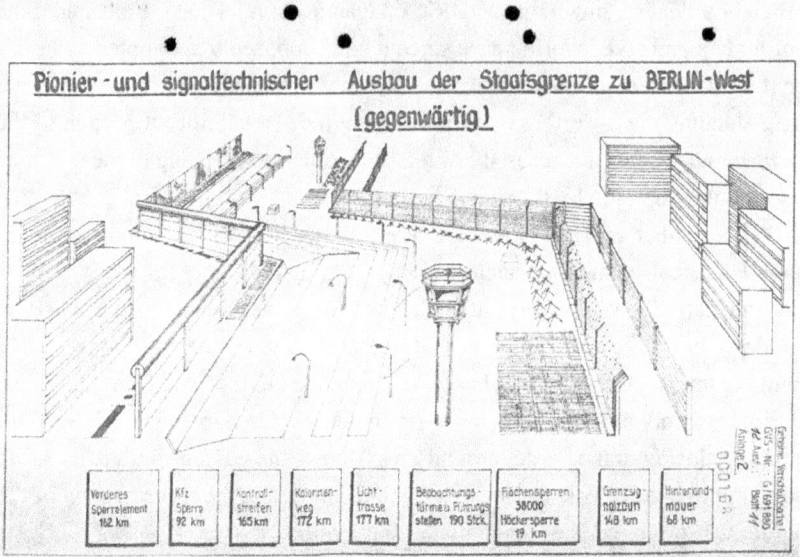

Figure 1 A schematic East German plan about the fortified border between East Berlin (right) and West Berlin (left) in the 1980s. Note that the wall is near the border line; it served as a visual obstacle to prevent Western eyes from preying.
Source: *Bundesarchiv*, DVH 32/127608.

The brutal measure of closing the West Berlin escape hatch was highly effective. The number of monthly escapees dropped from over 30,000 in July to around 1,000 six months later. Starting in June 1962, the GDR replaced its provisional walls dividing Berlin with pre-fab segments near the border line, tore down buildings on its side of the border line, and created a 30- to 100-meter-wide cleared zone zigzagging through divided Berlin. An update in 1965 added a rounded crown to the walls, making climbing over it almost impossible. Still, by the mid-1960s, the actual wall was only 15 kilometers long; the remainder of the border around West Berlin consisted of barbed wire fences and other tentative barriers. For reputational reasons, the GDR decided against laying mines at its West Berlin borders (Figure 1). Ultimately, the extended wall and the increasingly wider, cleared strip formed a scar running through the historically grown city. Apart from Gorizia at the Yugoslav–Italian border (see Section 3), it was the only Iron Curtain running through an urban environment. While one of Ulbricht's early biographers claimed that the GDR leader considered August 13, 1961, East Germany's "second birth," Khrushchev admitted three months later that it was an "ugly thing."[137]

---

[137] [Table for July 1961], no date, *Landesarchiv Berlin*, B Rep. 077, Nr. 652; "Aufstellung," no date, *Bundesarchiv Lichterfelde*, DC 20/12088, pg. 4; Rottman/Taylor, *Berlin Wall*, pp. 33, 42; Flemming, *Berliner Mauer*, pp. 97–98; Norbert Podewin, *Walter Ulbricht* (Dietz, 1995), p. 359

Despite the drop of successful escapes within months, breakthroughs still continued. Until the end of the year, an astounding 8,500 still managed to flee, although 3,400 were arrested and charged with the crime of *Republikflucht*. At the beginning, people jumped from windows of borderline houses before all openings were bricked up, and then from roof tops. Other escapees crashed cars or even trains through the initial barriers. For years, West Berlin activists operated flight tunnels. On August 22, 1961, the East German communist regime explicitly reconfirmed the shoot-to-kill order at the borders around West Berlin. Yet, the first person that had died at the newly fortified border was a woman who fell from a rooftop the previous day in an attempt to escape pursuing East Berlin policemen. But already on the 24th, a border guard killed a man with gunfire as he tried to swim to West Berlin. At least 140 people died at the Berlin Wall between August 13, 1961, and November 9, 1989 – over half of them by bullets fired by East German guards. Escapees, deserters, and friendly fire killed 8 border guards.[138]

The fortification of the border around West Berlin precipitated similar policies at the German–German border, which mostly so far had been secured only by a double fence of barbed wire, watchtowers, and a plowed strip. In consultation with the Soviet army, the GDR decided in mid-September of 1961 to lay mines at selected stretches of the border. In November, the regime also decreed the general improvement of fortifications at the entire German–German border, although it knew that its resources were not sufficient to build a Berlin-style wall along all of the 1,393 kilometers. Once more, citizens deemed unreliable – in total 3,175 – were expelled from their residences in the 5-kilometer restricted area along the border before the mid-1960s.[139]

Until 1989, the various obstacles at the borders around West Berlin and dividing Germany received periodical technical updates and replacements. In mid-1975, newly designed pre-fab elements appeared at either border, partially because they were easy to mass-produce. Still, the GDR never erected walls at its entire border with West Germany; in rural and sparsely populated regions, a cheaper-to-produce but rugged metal grid fence sufficed. But Berlin-style walls divided several rural settlements, like the tiny village of Mödlareuth at the

---

(first quote); "Report of the Ambassador of the Federal Republic of Germany in Moscow, Kroll," 11/9/1961, Deutschland, Bundesministerium des Innern, ed., *Dokumente zur Deutschlandpolitik*, ser. 4, vol. 7, part 2 (Oldenbourg, 1976), p. 925 (second quote).

[138] Führ, *Berliner Mauer*, p. 57; *Newsday*, 8/17/1961:1; *CDT*, 9/9/1961:4; *BG*, 12/6/1961:1; Arnold/Kellerhoff, *Unterirdisch*; Jochen Staadt, "Die DDR-Staatsgrenze West und ihre Bewacher," Klaus Schroeder and Jochen Staadt, *Die Grenze des Sozialismus in Deutschland* (Peter Lang, 2018), pp. 413–14; Hertle, *Die Todesopfer an der Berliner Mauer*, pp. 538–44.

[139] Meinke, "Zweimal," p. 57; Führ, *Berliner Mauer*, p. 81; Bennewitz/Potratz, *Zwangsaussiedlungen*, pp. 111–69, 284.

Thuringian-Bavarian border from 1966 to 1989. Unsurprisingly, the divided hamlet acquired the nickname 'Little Berlin.'[140]

Despite the increased East German fortification of its borders, GDR citizens still tried to escape. Between January 1, 1962, and April 10, 1965, over 2,700 East German citizens managed to escape with forged documents, more than 6,100 fled across the German–German border, and almost 2,800 to West Berlin. The annual number of successful escapes across both borders, however, sank to less than 100 in 1975, then increased to over 1,400 by 1983, fell again to less than 100 in 1987, before it increased once more to over a thousand until 1989. More and more, GDR citizens tried to escape via third countries, like Hungary, where the Iron Curtain was gradually becoming porous, as described in Section 7. In total, over 40,000 GDR citizens managed to cross the fortified borders between August 1961 and November 1989; more than 235,000 managed to flee in total. The ever-updated GDR border fortifications around West Berlin and dividing Germany required increasing inventiveness by potential escapees, even if many cases resemble similar attempts at the Hungarian and Czechoslovak border, as covered in previous sections. East German citizens walked across isolated and unmined border stretches, used airplanes to escape, flew a self-made hot air balloon across the border, drove a heavy construction caterpillar across detonating mines, dressed up in fake Allied uniforms, or were shuttled across the border hidden in cars.[141]

Even border guards, many of whom were young conscripts, fled in great numbers. Among the 10,756 members that escaped between January 1, 1950, and June 30, 1987, almost 2,500 deserted to West Berlin and West Germany after August 13, 1961. Throughout the period of Germany's division, the GDR had to withdraw thousands of conscripted men from the border service due to political unreliability, or in the wake of voluntary requests on ethical grounds. In the period from 1961 to 1989, at least 204 members of the border units committed suicide during service. Still, the border fortifications, including minefields, automatic self-shooting mechanisms, and vigilant border guards ultimately caused the death of at least 147 attempting to escape at the

---

[140] Rottman/Taylor, *Berlin Wall*, pp. 36–40; Gundlach, *Die Grenzüberwachung der DDR*, pp. 28–29, 32–33; on Mödlareuth: www.mdr.de/geschichte/ddr/mauer-grenze/moedlareuth-sperrgebiet-sperrzone-100.html, accessed on January 26, 2025.

[141] Staadt, "Die DDR-Staatsgrenze," pp. 460–64; Lochen, "Die geheimgehaltenen Bestimmungen," p. 20; *HC*, 3/7/1967:1a; flight in airplane: www.ddr-im-blick.de/jahrgaenge/jahrgang-1964/report/flucht-aus-der-ddr-mit-flugzeug/, accessed on January 26, 2025; *Newsday*, 9/17/1979:1Q; *JP*, 4/30/1982:4; *Bund*-e, 12/29/1965:16; *NZN*, 9/8/1979:2.

German–German border. At least 54 border guards died, some by gunfire fights with deserters and refugees but others also in accidents.[142]

The closing of the borders around West Berlin on August 13, 1961, cut families apart, severed crosstown friendships, and terminated professional relationships. West Berlin lost at one stroke 80,000 employees – around 6 percent its labor force – who had commuted from East Germany and East Berlin. Citizens of Western Allied countries still could visit East Berlin on the basis of Allied agreements dating to 1945. West German citizens were allowed to enter East Berlin again with a valid visa by August 23, 1961, but most West Berliners needed to obtain a residence permit; that is, they were required to move formally to East Berlin if they wanted to enter the communist half of the city. Only around 4,000 West Berliners who worked either for the East German-run railroad, S-Bahn, and U-Bahn systems, or for cultural establishments in East Berlin were allowed to enter without restrictions. In comparison, East German citizens were no longer able to enter West Berlin or West Germany legally. Those found on transit trains to West Germany in mid-August were forced to disembark before reaching the border, even if they had valid travel documents.[143]

In the years after August 1961, the governments of West Berlin and West Germany tried to negotiate a revision of the strict border regime to lessen its human toll, particularly for Berliners on either side of the wall. The GDR and West Berlin eventually agreed on a series of arrangements running from December 1963 to April 1966 that allowed West Berliners to visit their relatives in East Berlin for 24 hours during defined periods around Christmas, Easter, and Pentecost. Yet, most East Berliners were still not permitted to visit West Berlin. By November 1964, however, the GDR allowed its retired citizens to visit relatives in West Berlin and West Germany, obviously since their labor was no longer needed. The expectation which the regime may have entertained, that many would not return (and hence forfeit their retirement benefits), did not materialize. Of almost 650,000 retirees who traveled before the end of 1964, less than 200 did not come back.[144]

---

[142] Staadt, "Die DDR-Staatsgrenze," pp. 433–60, 465–68; Schroeder/Staadt, *Die Todesopfer*, pp. 642–63.

[143] *LAT*, 8/14/1961:1; *CDT*, 8/20/1961:5; *NZN*, 8/21/1961:5; *WP*, 8/21/1961:A5; *NZZ*-n, 8/23/1961:1; *AS*, 8/24/1961:B1; *SCMP*, 8/17/1961:1.

[144] Flemming, *Berliner Mauer*, pp. 109–15; Eckart Huhn, *Die Passierscheinvereinbarungen des Berliner Senats mit der Regierung der DDR 1963 bis 1966*, doctoral dissertation, Fern-Universität Hagen, 2009; various documents in: *Landesarchiv Berlin*, B Rep. 002 Nr. 13406 and 13406a; on retirees returning: www.ddr-im-blick.de/jahrgaenge/jahrgang-1965/report/private-reisen-von-ddr-rentnern-in-die-bundesrepublik/, accessed on January 26, 2025.

Although Soviet–American détente and German–German rapprochement between 1969 and 1972 had a major impact on the Cold War in general, it did not change the situation at the fortified borders, nor allow most of the East German citizens to exit. Apart from formalizing German–German governmental relations, détente and rapprochement, at a minimum, forced the two Germanys to regulate East German control of transit of civilians from West Germany to West Berlin by road, rail, and water – but not by air, which remained an Allied prerogative. In any case, as early as the end of August of 1961, the GDR had reconfirmed to the USSR that it would honor Western Allied transit rights. However, throughout the 1960s, East Germany used its de facto power to interrupt land transit several times, particularly when it wanted to exert political pressure on West Berlin or West Germany.[145]

In the 1980s, East Germany's accelerating economic decline and the Soviet inability to stop it forced the GDR to seek economic and financial assistance from its despised West German and capitalist sibling. The removal of mines from the German–German border in 1983 and improvements in the treatment of entering and exiting West German citizens at border crossing and transit points were among the first concessions by the East German regime. Further concessions included a significant increase of occasions on which East German citizens younger than 65 were allowed to visit West German family from the very restricted list in the original 1972 regulations.[146] Yet, the fortifications of the borders remained in place until late 1989.

The brutality of the GDR border regime at the Iron Curtain in Europe as well as East Germany's dismal economic performance by the late 1980s prepared the groundswell of popular dissatisfaction that eventually toppled the communist regime in late 1989. The removal of the last vestiges of the Iron Curtain at the Hungarian–Austrian border since May, as described in the previous section, opened the possibility for renewed mass escapes. Over the summer, Hungarian border guards still tried to stop and send back East German tourists who tried to escape to West Germany via Austria. Still, an increasing number of GDR citizens refused to return to their home country but instead decided to wait in Hungary for a new opportunity. Eventually, on September 11, Hungary opened the border; within days, 57,000 GDR citizens left for West Germany. Since August, East German tourists in Czechoslovakia had also occupied the West German embassy in Prague in the hope of receiving permission to emigrate to the Federal Republic. After

---

[145] Lüthi, *Cold Wars*, p. 433; "Für Genossen Kegel," 8/24/1961, *Bundesarchiv Lichterfelde*, DY 30/3509, p. 34; *BT*, 2/14/1969:7.

[146] Gundlach, *Die Grenzüberwachung der DDR*, pp. 24–25; Klaus Schroeder, *Der SED Staat* (Carl Hanser, 1998), p. 258; *NZZ*, 2/13/1982:3; *NZZ*, 12/30/1986:3; *NZZ*, 4/1/1989:4.

negotiations between the two Germanys, 4,000 citizens in the embassy were allowed to leave on September 30. As tens of thousands of GDR citizens left via third countries, including the West German embassy in Poland, mass demonstrations calling for political reforms gathered momentum in East Germany itself. On October 18, long-term communist leader Erich Honecker resigned under pressure from his own Politburo colleagues. Facing mass demonstrations on the street, the communist party announced suddenly on November 9, 1989, the opening of borders and unrestricted travel abroad. Unprepared and uninformed, border guards opened within hours the barriers at crossing points at the Berlin Wall under pressure from thousands of GDR citizens demanding to be allowed to pass immediately. Within days, border crossing points along the entire length of the German–German border opened up as well. The East German Iron Curtain tumbled peacefully within days in the second week of November. The GDR followed within less than a year. On October 3, 1990, communist Germany ceased to exist when it acceded to the Federal Republic of Germany.[147]

9 Other Iron Curtains

The other external borders of the Socialist Camp displayed a remarkably wide range of different characteristics. The vast majority ran through uninhabited or mountainous territory, which made fortifications less important, or through the seas, which could not be easily secured. Still, a few stretches witnessed massive refugee streams, while other areas were heavily safeguarded. In many cases, tensions at the land borders decreased after Stalin's death in 1953, with cooperation in joint border projects starting only a little later. Space and the lack of specialized literature does not allow but for a cursory sketch of Iron Curtains in northern Europe, the Balkans, the Caucasus, the border lines from the Caspian Sea to the Southeast Asia, the boundaries of Macao and Hong Kong, the Demilitarized Zone of Korea, and the maritime borders.

*

The Nordic Iron Curtain separating the USSR from Finland and Norway ran from the Baltic Sea to the Arctic Sea through mostly uninhabited lake and tundra landscapes (Map 11). After World War II, Finland lost half of Karelia in the southeast, Salla in the east, and Petsamo at the Arctic Sea. Even if the Paris Peace Treaty formalized these territorial changes only by early 1947, Finland and the USSR had started to demarcate the new 1,340-kilometer-long border line as early as mid-1945. In the late 1940s, a 10-meter-wide cleared and plowed

---
[147] Taylor, *Berlin Wall*, pp. 430–54; Flemming, *Berliner Mauer*, pp. 176–90.

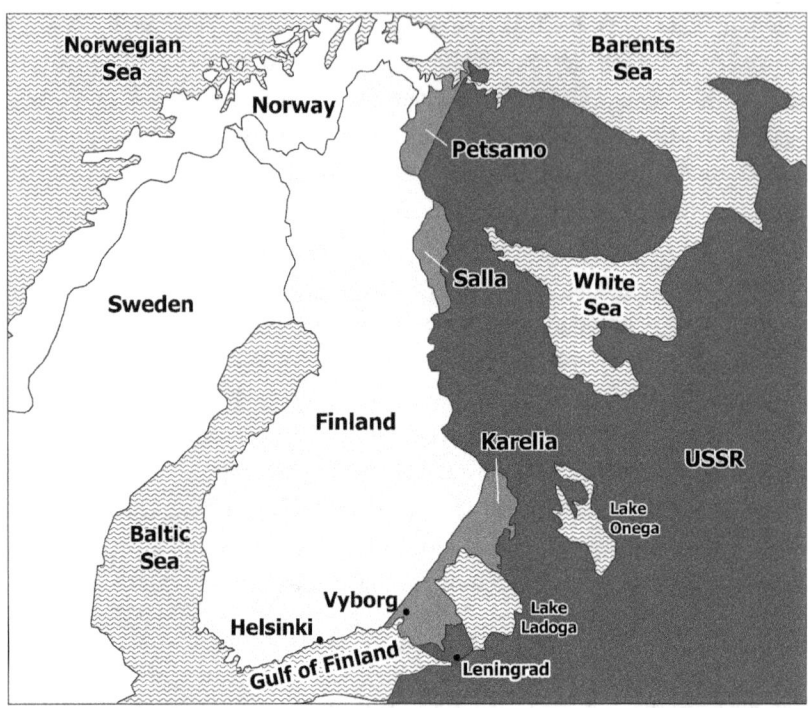

Map 11 The Nordic Iron Curtain. Finland's territorial losses (grey); its loss of access to the Arctic Sea created the Soviet–Norwegian border.

strip with a double barbed wire fence marked the border. From the western side, observers could make out abandoned farmsteads, formerly owned by Finns and Karelians, across the boundary line. One of only three at the entire border, the crossing point on the road from Helsinki to Vyborg (Viipuri) neither experienced much traffic, nor was well guarded. It was only open by day for diplomatic traffic and, in the summer, for a few Finnish tourists. By agreement, Finland was supposed to return any Soviet escapee who managed to cross the lightly guarded border. An American newspaper article claimed in 1966 that this Iron Curtain was "one of the most peaceful and relaxed between the West and the Communist world."[148]

The calm but tight Soviet–Finnish Cold War border opened slightly on January 1, 1970, after the two neighbors had agreed on visa-free tourist travel for its citizens, beating Hungary and Austria by nine years (see Section 7). By the

---

[148] John H. Wuorinen, "The Finnish Treaty," *The Annals of the American Academy of Political and Social Science*, 257 (1948), p. 92; FOIA Reading Room: CIA-RDP08C01297R000500010011-6, p. 27; *CDT*, 9/30/1948:17; *Observer*, 2/26/1950:5; *NYT*, 9/27/1955:11; *CT*, 11/3/1963:A3; *CT*, 9/11/1966:B22; *AA*, 12/4/1966:A10 (quote).

spring, the USSR also allowed visa-free travel for Western tourists to Leningrad (St. Petersburg) on Finnish hotel ships. Yet, for many Soviet citizens a visit to Finland or even emigration remained out of reach. By the 1970s, the border had become significantly fortified with watchtowers, trip wires, and guard dogs on the Soviet side. A few escapees still managed to cross in the wild north and continue hiking through northern Finland to Sweden in an attempt to avoid arrest and repatriation to the USSR. Escapees often could rely on sympathetic locals who offered food, shelter, and maps for their onward journey.[149]

The USSR gained Norway as a new neighbor at the Arctic circle as a result of Finland's loss of Petsamo after World War II. The signing of the North Atlantic Treaty in May 1949 turned the 196-kilometer-long new border into the first Soviet boundary with the hostile Western alliance. By 1946, Norway and the USSR had agreed on the exact border line; in late 1947, demarcation on the ground had been concluded. The border did not have a single official crossing point. Its non-fortified boundary line was marked only by twin border posts, although the USSR erected a series of watchtowers 200 meters inland by the early 1950s. Hence, grazing Norwegian cows recurrently strayed into the Soviet borderlands during the summer. Barbed wire fences appeared on the Soviet side only by the early 1970s. Despite its light fortification, barely any escape attempt occurred at this Soviet border.[150]

This Soviet–NATO border in the high north was remarkably peaceful, too. A 1949 border activities agreement regulated fishing in the border rivers. Norwegians were allowed to wade to the border-line in mid-river; beyond, they risked a spray of Soviet bullets. The NATO border soon became an international tourist destination with overly audacious thrill seekers trying to dip their feet across the boundary line. Despite being on opposite sides of the Cold War, Norway and the USSR cooperated in the construction of the hydroelectrical plant *Borisoglebsky* (across from Storskog) on the Paatsjoki River in 1955–65. This rather peaceful cohabitation was interrupted only in June 1968, when the USSR sent tanks to the border line in retaliation for NATO maneuvers in central Norway. Within less than ten years, the two sides agreed to mark the ear lobes of Norwegian reindeer herds that frequently crossed over the newly erected but often snow-covered border fences. Norwegian herders were allowed to cross into Soviet territory on snowmobiles to drive their animals back west. On the Soviet side, reindeer herding was

---

[149] The agreement of 10/18/1969 is available in: United Nations, *Treaty Series*, vol. 675 (United Nations, 1972), pp. 108–20; *BG*, 3/15/1970:A23; *LAT*, 9/30/1979:G1; *GM*, 10/7/1980:5; *LAT*, 12/16/1980:C7; *Sun*, 3/13/1983:A2.

[150] *NZZ*-e, 8/21/1946:5; *HC*, 8/26/1962:24A; *CSM*, 10/22/1962:9; *Scotsman*, 5/9/1959:12; *Guardian*, 4/3/1974:12.

no longer practiced after settlements in the border region had been abandoned in the late 1940s.[151]

*

The Balkan Iron Curtain cut through Southeast Europe from the Adriatic Sea to the Black Sea (Map 12). Greece's Cold War borders to Albania, Yugoslavia (today's North Macedonia), and Bulgaria ran mostly through mountainous areas. Only the eastern end of the Bulgarian-Greek border and the whole Bulgarian-Turkish border were lying in flat river valleys and forested hillscapes. Historically, almost the entire boundary line had been contested after the start of the gradual collapse of Ottoman Empire in the mid-nineteenth century. Competing territorial claims, particularly around triple-divided Macedonia, continued into the post–World War II period. In 1945, Tito entertained the idea of creating a Greater Yugoslavia with Albania and Bulgaria.[152] Over the course of the second half of the 1940s, Greece's three communist neighbors provided the Greek communists with staging and recuperation places for the civil war against the constitutional government of postwar Greece.

The 228-kilometer-long Yugoslav–Greek border was Europe's most unusual in the pantheon of Iron Curtains. Fleeing the outbreak of civil war, Greek

Map 12 The Balkan and Caucasian Iron Curtains. After World War II, the Soviet Union entertained territorial designs on Turkey's northeastern provinces and on Iranian (Persian) Azerbaijan.

---

[151] CIA-RDP08C01297R000500010011-6, pages 6, 19; *NYT*, 4/26/1953:X25; Felix Frey, "A Fluid Iron Curtain," *Scandinavian Journal of History*, 45/4 (2020), pp. 506–26; *Guardian*, 6/10/1968:9; *HC*, 4/24/1977:20A.
[152] *NYT*, 7/15/1945:17.

Macedonians crossed into Yugoslav Macedonia as early as 1944. The elected Greek government eventually suppressed the communist guerillas after it had received American military help in the wake of Truman's proclamation of his famous doctrine on March 12, 1947. In June 1949, a year after the split with the USSR, Yugoslavia closed the border to Greek fighters in the hope of obtaining Western economic assistance. In mid-October, the defeated Greek communists announced a cease-fire. Within a week, Yugoslavia expressed its interest in restoring good neighborly relations with its former Cold War enemy to the south. By late 1950, Belgrade released Greek soldiers it had held as prisoners of war and returned Greek children it had seized. By early 1951, the two sides opened a rebuilt rail link, and by late 1952, they completed border demarcation on the ground.[153] In the wake of Greece's and Turkey's accession to NATO in February 1952, Tito's Yugoslavia even pushed for a friendship treaty and trilateral military alliance, which were eventually signed days before Stalin's death and the following year, respectively.[154] Given the strict Yugoslav passport regulations in place since 1948 (see Section 3), the pacified border to Greece still witnessed its share of Yugoslav refugees crossing over the course of the 1950s, though never at the level occurring at Yugoslavia's northwestern borders. The end of Yugoslavia's strict passport regime in 1959 and the subsequent de facto amnesty of citizens who had left illegally since 1948 turned the Yugoslav–Greek Iron Curtain finally into an ordinary border. By the 1970s, local border traffic, commerce, and personal ties were flourishing.[155]

The 282-kilometer-long Albanian-Greek Iron Curtain cut through an ethnically mixed border region that left a significant Greek minority in Albania and a smaller Albanian minority in Greece. During the civil war, Greek communist fighters received political and military support from Albania as well. The closure of the Yugoslav border in June 1949 turned anti-Yugoslav Albania for a short while into the major supporter of the Greek communist rebels. Yet, after the end of the Greek Civil War, the mountainous Albanian-Greek border quickly lost its military significance. Over the course of the 1950s, Albanian farmer families managed to escape with herds across the patrolled but unfortified border.[156] In the first half of the 1960s, the communist country returned several groups of hostages whom the retreating Greek guerillas had taken before 1949. Greece's formal repudiation of its territorial claims in southern Albania in early 1971 led to the reestablishment of

---

[153] Spyridon Plakoudas, *The Greek Civil War* (I.B. Tauris, 2017); *GM*, 10/24/1949:16; *DBG*, 11/8/1950:31; *Tat*, 11/27/1950:2; *NZZ*-m, 2/17/1951:2; *CDT*, 10/29/1952:17.

[154] Evanthis Hatzivassiliou, "Coping with the Regional Cold War," Martin Previšić, ed., *Rethinking the Cold War* (De Gruyter, 2021), p. 66.

[155] *NZZ*-m, 8/16/1958:5; *NZZ*-e, 7/14/1961:5; *NYT*, 4/18/1976:11.

[156] *HT*, 6/26/1949:11; *SCMP*, 8/7/1950:10; *DBG*, 11/15/1956:40; *CSM*, 3/18/1959:14.

bilateral diplomatic relations that had been interrupted since 1940. In early 1985, the two sides reopened the highway between the two countries after 35 years of closure. On this occasion, mostly ethnic Greek relatives, who had not seen each other for a whole generation, were allowed to meet for the day. However, the road subsequently was open only to diplomatic and commercial traffic. The last European communist regime to fall, Albania opened its tightly guarded borders only in January 1990.[157] An internal Albanian government report from late that year claimed that a mere 13,602 people had fled between 1944 and 1989, of whom 988 had died. Families of refugees considered these numbers too low.[158]

In the immediate post–World War II period, the 494-kilometer-long Bulgarian-Greek Iron Curtain witnessed defense fortifications and restricted border areas on the Bulgarian side, communist cross-border support for Greek guerilla forces, a bilateral arms race, territorial disputes, and the complete lack of diplomatic relations. The end of the Greek Civil War did not lead to a reduction of tensions, however. In the early 1950s, the two sides used military force in their contest over three small islands in the Maritsa River at the eastern end of the border. With Greece's and Turkey's accession to NATO, Bulgaria's entire southern border became one long dividing line between the hostile Cold War blocs. Yet, after Stalin's death in March 1953, Bulgaria, too, reached out to Greece to improve relations, acquiring a boundary line agreement (including the equitable distribution of the contested islands) later in the year and returning Greek prisoners taken in the civil war the following year.[159] In 1964, both sides formally dropped all territorial claims against each other. But despite these signs of relaxation, both countries maintained their military posture and kept up security zones with restricted access for non-residents. Still, in 1952, the Kulata crossing point at the western border sector exhibited only a barbed wire fence at the boundary line with a jungle of 10-foot-high reeds in the strip behind.[160] In the mid-1970s, after the end of the Greek military dictatorship and in view of the Greek–Turkish conflict over Cyprus, the democratically elected government in Athens sought to improve cultural and economic relations with Sofia, but the border never experienced the kind of normality that had emerged at the Yugoslav–Greek border after 1959. On the contrary, Bulgarian border guards recurrently shot and killed both Greek citizens

---

[157] *NZZ*-n, 6/26/1961:2; *NZZ*-n, 12/29/1961:2; *NZZ*-n, 8/12/1964:2; *NYT*, 11/14/1971:2; *IT*, 1/14/1984:5; *CT*, 7/14/1990:D1.

[158] Jonila Godole and Valbona Bezati, "'In the People's Service' – Border policy in communist Albania," https://konferencashkencore.wordpress.com/wp-content/uploads/2020/02/jonila-godole-valbona-bezati-e2809cin-the-peoples-servicee2809d-border-policy-in-communist-albania.pdf, accessed July 30, 2025.

[159] *HT*, 7/14/1945:5; *NZZ*-e, 7/17/1945:2; *NZZ*-n, 10/11/1950:1; *NZZ*, 1/1/1954:2; *NZZ*-e, 10/13/1954:2.

[160] *NYT*, 9/30/1964:3; *CT*, 4/19/1965:C6; *MG*, 12/16/1952:6.

straying into unsecured mountainous Bulgarian border territory and escapees trying to exit.[161]

The 259-kilometer-long Bulgarian-Turkish border turned out to be the most hazardous among the four Balkan Iron Curtains. In October 1945, Soviet occupation troops in Bulgaria moved to the boundary line in an act of intimidation related to Stalin's concurrent territorial demands at the Dardanelles and in northeastern Turkey (see also later). Over the course of the second half of the 1940s, the Soviet military administration in Bulgaria and then the new communist regime there periodically closed the border, either in the wake of denying exit visas to Bulgarian citizens, or to suppress smuggling, or in reaction to the Truman Doctrine. By the late 1940s, Bulgaria also established a restricted border zone to stop illegal exit, while Turkey set up a layered defense along the entire border in expectation of Communist military aggression. In the early 1950s, Bulgaria's actual Iron Curtain to Turkey mainly consisted of a barbed wire fence and minefields; as at other Iron Curtains, rainstorms frequently dislodged mines and killed unsuspecting Turkish soldiers on patrol. Similar to Soviet and Czech minority policies in the interwar and postwar period (see Sections 1–2 and 5), Bulgaria also expelled some parts of its Muslim population to Turkey in the 1950–52 period.[162] After Stalin's death, Sofia tried to relax relations with Ankara as well, but the border remained a location of recurrent incidents, including cross-border firefights. Still, Bulgarian border guards as well civilians, including East German citizens, attempted to flee across the border to Turkey, sometimes with deadly results.[163] In the mid-1960s, Sofia tried to relax relations with Ankara further, resulting in a 1967 agreement on the peaceful resolution of border incidents. Subsequently, the border remained largely out of the limelight of politics and media, mainly due to the rising tensions between Bulgaria's NATO neighbors Greece and Turkey. When the failing Bulgarian communist regime played the nationalist card in the 1980s to shore up sagging support among the Slavic majority population, harassment of Muslim citizens once more intensified. Starting in mid-decade, Bulgarian Muslims escaped persecution across the Iron Curtain to Turkey, sometimes via Greece. When Sofia expelled up to 300,000 Muslim citizens in three months after late May 1989, relations between the two countries soured quickly. As this chauvinist and misguided policy deprived Bulgaria's economy of urgently

---

[161] *NZZ*, 1/13/1976:3; *NZZ*, 9/19/1983:4.
[162] *NZZ*-m, 10/23/1945:1; *CDT*, 3/15/1946:3; *NZZ*-m, 3/10/1947:2; *NZZ*-m, 11/22/1948:2; *WP*, 8/24/1951:C7; *NZZ*-n, 7/1/1953:2; *NZZ*-m, 11/21/1950:2; *NZZ*-m, 11/11/1952:5.
[163] *NZZ*-n, 8/31/1953:2; *NZZ*-n, 5/18/1954:2; *NZZ*-m, 7/13/1955:2; *NZZ*-m, 6/21/1958:2; *NZZ*-e, 1/14/1957:2; *NZZ*-e, 7/21/1961:5; *NZZ*-e, 9/17/1962:2.

needed labor, it turned out to be one of the causes for the collapse of communist rule in November of 1989.[164]

*

The Caucasian Iron Curtain separated the Soviet Union from Turkey and Iran between the Black Sea and the Caspian Sea (Map 12). Like in Central Europe and the Balkans, it also split local populations in ethnically mixed regions, particularly Turks, Kurds, Armenians, and Azeris. In 1952, Turkish accession to NATO turned the shared border into the second Soviet boundary with the hostile Western alliance, following the border with Norway in 1949 (see discussion earlier). Conflict at the Soviet border with Iran mostly revolved around competing territorial claims.

The 601-kilometer-long border that separated Turkey from the Soviet Socialist Republics Georgia, Armenia, and Azerbaijan ran from the Black Sea through mountains, flat highlands, and lakes as well as along an extended stretch of the Aras River to the Soviet–Iranian border. At the end of World War II, the USSR laid claim to two provinces in northeastern Turkey (Ardahan and Kars), initiating one of the earliest Cold War crises. Even if Stalin eventually backed off in the face of determined Western counterpressure, the episode led Truman to include Turkey as a recipient of military and economic aid in his doctrine in March 1947. The USSR formally repudiated its territorial claims only after Stalin's death. In any case, since 1944, ethnic Turks, Kurds, and Greeks had been forcefully removed from the Soviet Caucasus for a second time after 1935–38; deportations continued to 1949.[165] By mid-1947, the Turkish–Soviet border comprised one open border crossing point that handled road traffic and a few trains per week, but otherwise was heavily militarized at its entire length on both sides. The actual border line sported a barbed wire fence on the Soviet side, watchtowers in the adjacent cleared and plowed strip, and another 8-kilometer-wide border area from which all residents had been removed. Still, Soviet citizens recurrently managed to dodge Soviet bullets by night and escape in the late 1940s. The tense border remained a place of intermittent low-level armed clashes throughout the entire Cold War, leading Turkey in 1967 to demand from NATO the delivery of nuclear mines [sic!] for defensive purposes. Legal cross-border travel for citizens from either side remained impossible until the 1980s, when elderly Soviet citizens were finally allowed to visit relatives in Turkey once every five years.[166]

---

[164] *NZZ*-e, 5/7/1965:5; *NZZ*, 12/19/1965:6; *NZZ*-n, 12/29/1967:1; *NZZ*, 4/17/1985:4; Lüthi, *Cold Wars*, p. 588.

[165] Jamil Hasanli, *Stalin and the Turkish Crisis of the Cold War, 1945–1953* (Rowman & Littlefield, 2011); *Bund*-m, 6/12/1953:1; Nikolai Bougai, *Deportation of Peoples in the SU* (Nova, 1996), pp. 47–49, 131–49.

[166] *CDT*, 6/20/1947:3; *Sun*, 8/24/1947:A1; *HC*, 11/10/1957:2B; *NYT*, 8/23/1959:4; *NYT*, 8/18/1962:2; *CT*, 10/3/1967:14; *LAT*, 11/17/1985:6.

By 1968, Ankara's difficult relationship with its NATO allies Greece and the United States had triggered a low level of economic rapprochement with Moscow. From 1976 to 1981, the two countries even cooperated in the construction of a jointly operated hydroelectrical dam at the Akhuryan (Arpachay) border river.[167] Still, the heavily fortified border that, by then, even included high-voltage electrical fences, remained tense until the late 1980s, although it continued to witness frequent Soviet escapes. In 1988, following eighteen years of negotiations, the two sides permanently reopened the road along the Black Sea at the divided village of Sarpi (Sarp) for commercial and private travel. For the first time in over half a century, local relatives from both sides met again.[168]

Iran's border with Soviet Armenia and Azerbaijan (including the Azeri enclave Nakhchivan in Armenia) ran for 733 kilometers from the Turkish border mostly along the Aras River, through the Mughan Steppe, and across the Talish Mountains to the Caspian Sea. Stalin had territorial ambitions here as well – particularly in Iran's northwestern province of Persian (Iranian) Azerbaijan – but backed off in the face of determined Iranian and Western resistance.[169] By the late 1940s, the entire Soviet–Iranian border, including the sector east of the Caspian Sea (now the Iranian–Turkmen border), was heavily militarized on both sides. Surprisingly, the hotspot in the early 1950s was not in the flat Mughan Steppe but Julfa on the Aras River. Its railroad bridge linked the two namesake villages on either side; it had been a key avenue of invasion from the north since 1910. The settlement on the Soviet side (in the Azeri Nakhchivan enclave) sported barbed wire, border guards, watchtowers, and search lights. In the early 1950s, loudspeakers warned Iran that it would be next after the US defeat in the concurrent Korean War. Yet, as early as 1950, Moscow sought a boundary agreement to defuse tensions; negotiations started after Stalin's death and led to an agreement and demarcation on the ground by 1957. Still, the loudspeaker war at Julfa continued. When Iran tried to take up a more even-handed position in the Cold War in the 1960s, both countries cooperated in the construction of joint hydroelectrical dam upriver from Julfa. However, after the Iranian Revolution in 1979, border tensions between the Islamic Republic and the USSR increased once more.[170] In early January of 1990, thousands of Shiites residing in the Nakhchivan enclave tore down barbed wire fences on the banks of the Aras River, destroyed watchtowers, dismantled electronic

---

[167] *Scotsman*, 7/15/1968:7.
[168] Mathijs Pelkmans, *Defending the Border* (Cornell University Press, 2006), pp. 22–25, 27–39; Scott, *Defectors*, pp. 91–96.
[169] Hasanli, *Stalin*, pp. 123–73.
[170] *SCMP*, 8/31/1949:5; *CDT*, 8/19/1950:11; *CDT*, 8/21/1950:A2; *MG*, 8/16/1952:4; *NYT*, 2/27/1957:7; *SCMP*, 6/30/1959:11; *SCMP*, 12/15/1966:14; Mehrunnisa Ali, "Iran's Relations with the US and the USSR," *Pakistan Horizon*, 26/3 (1973), p. 52; *LAT*, 6/22/1990:A1.

equipment, and interrupted communication lines in protest against their continued, forced separation from their religious and ethnic relatives in Iran. KGB and army units eventually suppressed the uprising.[171] With the collapse of the USSR, the border lost its military significance and installations.

*

The southern border of the USSR and the People's Republic of China (PRC) ran from the Caspian Sea through mostly uninhabited territory along the Turkmen-Khorasan Mountain Range, through the southeastern Karakum Desert, in the fairways of multiple rivers, and roughly along the Himalayan crestline to Southeast Asia. At its eastern end, the Iron Curtain frayed into several strands at different points in time. From 1949 to 1954, the Iron Curtain followed the Chinese border to the South China Sea; between 1954 and 1975, it turned south at meeting point of the Sino-Vietnamese-Laotian borders, and followed North Vietnam's border to Laos to the Demilitarized Zone at the 17th parallel, which cut Vietnam into two halves. From 1975 to the end of the Cold War, the Iron Curtain followed the Laotian and Cambodian western borders with Burma (Myanmar) and Thailand from China to the Gulf of Thailand. Reliable data about this long, multinational border is still very scarce. During the Soviet intervention in Afghanistan between 1979 and 1989, for example, the USSR extended its border regime into the neighboring country to prevent Mujahidin attacks in Central Asia.[172] The Tibetan–Indian border in the Himalayas was relatively open for local border crossings until 1959; after the Chinese suppression of the Tibetan uprising, it became heavily militarized.[173] Since the North Vietnamese–Laotian border was poorly guarded, the communist regime in Hanoi used Laotian territory for its famous Ho-Chi-Minh Trail to supply guerilla forces in South Vietnam.[174] Throughout the Cold War, Southeast Asia experienced massive refugee streams across its various land borders which however were mostly related to war and ethnic persecution.[175]

Finally, East Asia sported three distinct Iron Curtains. At the Pearl River Delta, the British colony of Hong Kong and the Portuguese colony of Macao had been destinations for over 700,000 Chinese refugees between the restart of the Chinese Civil War in 1945 and communist victory in 1949. From 1951 to 1978, the PRC prohibited emigration, but Chinese citizens still managed to

---

[171] *CSM*, 1/4/1990:4; *Scotsman*, 1/4/1990:7; *NYT*, 1/7/1990:14; *LAT*, 1/15/1990:P1.
[172] Timothy Nunan, "The Violence Curtain," *Transcultural Studies*, 8/1 (2017), pp. 224–58.
[173] Reed H. Chervin, *The Cold War in the Himalayas* (Amsterdam University Press, 2024).
[174] John Prados, *The Blood Road* (Wiley, 1999).
[175] W. Courtland Robinson, *Terms of Refuge* (Zed Books, 1998), pp. 10–28, 66–126.

reach either colony through bribery, human smuggling, false pretenses, in search of medical care, or for other reasons. By 1953, two million refugees from mainland China lived in Hong Kong.[176] Unlike the colonial-turned-Cold War borders of coastal southern China, the Iron Curtain dividing Korea since armistice in 1953 remains the last Cold War border to this day. This Demilitarized Zone is an armistice line flanked by heavily militarized border zones on either side. According to South Korean data, only 607 North Koreans fled south until 1989, although the numbers increased to a total of over ten thousand in the following two decades. The digging of tunnels from North Korea and the establishment of a wall on the South Korean side may look similar to the situation in Berlin after 1961, but the purpose of either was primarily military – to infiltrate the south from the north, and to defend South Korea against a North Korean attack, respectively.[177]

*

Ultimately, a particular form of Iron Curtain ran along the multiple shorelines of the Socialist Camp. Unlike the flat *Neusiedler See* that sported a Hungarian fence for a while, seascapes do not lend themselves to fortifications, except on or near the coast. Poland surveilled and restricted access to its seashores, and the USSR built up a layered border regime with barbed wire and plowed strips at the Baltic coast.[178] Elsewhere, socialist states fell back on traditional naval means to identify and intercept escape attempts, which naturally was far less effective than controlling land borders. Probably over a million individuals managed to escape the entire Socialist Camp from 1945 to 1989, either by jumping ship in harbors, swimming, riding surfboards, or sailing by boats in virtually all seas from Europe to Asia.[179] Good statistics on maritime escapes during the Cold War exist mainly for East Germany and unified Vietnam. Of the 5,600 East German citizens who tried to cross the Baltic Sea to West Germany or Denmark between 1961 and 1989, only around 900 succeeded while at least 135 died and the rest were arrested.[180] Most tried to escape as individuals or in small groups. In comparison, almost eight hundred thousand people, the majority with Chinese ancestry, fled Vietnam in wooden boats holding up to one hundred and more people across the South China Sea to Hong Kong, the Philippines,

---

[176] Lili Song, *Chinese Refugee Law and Policy* (Cambridge University Press, 2020), pp. 132–34, 156–57; Laura Madokoro, *Elusive Refugee* (Harvard University Press, 2016), pp. 34–42.

[177] Daniel Schwekendiek, "A Meta-Analysis of North Koreans to China and South Korea," Frank Rüdiger, James E. Hoare, Patrick Köllner, and Susan Pares, eds., *Korea 2010* (Brill, 2010), p. 248; Kim Hyung-geun, *The DMZ* (Korea Foundation, 2010).

[178] Lars Fredrik Stöcker, *Bridging the Baltic Sea* (Lexington, 2018), pp. 71–72.

[179] Scott, *Defectors*, pp. 162, 174.

[180] Henning Hochstein, Jenny Linek, and Merete Peetz, *Tödliche Ostseefluchten aus der DDR 1961–1989* (Landeszentrale für politische Bildung Mecklenburg-Vorpommern, 2025).

Indonesia, Malaysia, and Thailand in the wake of Vietnamese reunification in 1976. Numerous attempts failed due to inclement weather, piracy, or Vietnamese naval interception. Around 10–15 percent perished at sea.[181]

Conclusions

The European borders of the Socialist Camp to the non-socialist world were almost unique in modern history. Their primary purpose was to keep people in, for economic, legal, and/or political reasons. In many respects, these secured borders were extensions of attempts by socialist regimes to regulate and control the lives of their own people. Citizens had no inherent right to determine the course and location of their own lives unless they helped the construction of a socialist state. The Soviet model of secured borders, as it had emerged in the interwar period, served as inspiration and sometimes as a paradigm for the socialist border regimes in Europe. However, the individual needs of socialist states there resulted in border regimes at variance in nature and periodical appearance. All socialist governments reserved the right to use lethal force to keep citizens in. The fortified border line was the last of a layered system of control. Strict passport and exit visa regulations as well as the surveillance of the population served to deter, discourage, and discover any attempt to flee. Removal or expulsion of suspect populations, access restrictions to the border area, and fortifications of all kinds in the border zone and at the border line acted as final lines of prevention. In general, the socialist border regimes in Europe moved through three development stages. In the intermediate post–World War II period, border security was far from effective, even though the emerging socialist regimes in East Europe tried to impose some form of exit control. From the late 1940s to the post-Stalinist period, border security was strict – with the exception of East Germany. After the mid-1950s, developments widely diverged between Yugoslavia, Hungary, the CSSR, and the GDR. East Germany was an extreme case both as a latecomer and as a builder of fortified borders.

The comparison of the socialist border regimes in Europe still reveals several unifying themes. Large numbers of citizens fled for a variety of reasons despite massive efforts by communist governments to the contrary; some socialist states like Yugoslavia in the 1950s and Hungary since the 1960s were willing to tolerate a certain level of illegal exit. Suspect populations, which were forcefully removed from border areas, almost always were ethnic minorities with historical contacts on the other side of the border, with the exception of

---

[181] Robinson, *Terms of Refuge*, pp. 28–32, 60–62, 166–71, 189–93, 294; Nghia M. Vo, *The Vietnamese Boat People, 1954 and 1975–1992* (McFarland, 2015), p. 167.

East Germany. On the basis of the available East German and Czechoslovak statistics, the number of illegal border transgressors killed by the shoot-to-kill order was surprisingly low, even if every single case was tragic and unnecessary. In a narrow sense, the legal and physical means to prevent escapes at the border were working; yet hundreds of thousands still managed to leave. Socialist governments felt compelled to modernize their border fortifications repeatedly to stop the outflow of dissatisfied people. The fortified socialist borders were also very dangerous and even lethal to border guards and local populations across the boundary line.

Most Iron Curtains have disappeared after the end of the Cold War. In the case of Europe, almost all formerly socialist countries, except Russia, Belarus, and Ukraine, have become members of NATO and/or the European Union. Passport-free travel across the former Iron Curtain is now the norm, not just a utopian dream. The only Iron Curtain that still exists has divided Korea since 1953. The Russian aggression against Ukraine since February 2022 has turned the relatively open border to Finland and the Baltic states into a tight border, but no Iron Curtain so far has reemerged.

What is left of the various Iron Curtains? In general, the Iron Curtain is a forgotten episode in the history of borders in most places. Only in Germany, an extensive memory culture has emerged. The country's traumatic division was, in some respects, a defining moment in the self-identity formation of the Federal Republic, which survived the Cold War and absorbed the GDR in 1990. The Berlin Wall and the adjacent death strip were quickly dismantled and turned into a combined hiking/bike path with educational displays and memorial plaques. The former German–German border is nowadays less visible, particularly in places dedicated to ecological conservation.[182] Official and private memorial sites dot the line where the walls and fences used to stand. The historiography on the East German and West Berlin border is well developed, primarily because German federal and state governments have invested much money in its historical exploration. And Berlin's tourism industry exploits the macabre history of the Cold War, and of the Nazi period, to great financial benefit. At other Iron Curtains, however, the memory culture is far less developed, though governments, universities, and museums in Bavaria, Austria, the Czech Republic, and Slovakia have sponsored a small number of historical projects and exhibits in the first twenty years after the end of the Cold War.

After 1989, overcoming the trauma of the Iron Curtain was at the center of legal and local initiatives in several European countries. During the 1990s and the early 2000s, state governments in Germany and the Federal Republic

---

[182] Pieck, *Mnemonic Ecologies*.

prosecuted East German border guards, who had killed refugees and bystanders. Four hundred fifty were indicted; two-thirds received light prison sentences, often on probation. Yet, there is an enduring sense of injustice because the big fish – the party, government, and military leaders who had signed and enforced the shoot-to-kill orders – often escaped legal consequences due to age or death, while the small fish, who had been young conscripts or subaltern officers at the time, were sentenced.[183] In the case of Albania, former high-ranking communist officials faced trials for the killings of refugees in 1990 and early 1991.[184] In the Czech Republic, the first trial occurred only in 2023 [sic!], but the accused former interior minister died at the age of 92 before sentencing.[185] With the end of the Cold War, border communities tried to reestablish long-suspended contacts, particularly at the former German–German border, at the Hungarian–Austrian border, and in the Caucasus. Due to the expulsion of the *Sudetendeutsche* after World War II, communities at the Czech border to Austria and Germany had first to get acquainted with each other as no historical contacts existed.[186] To many witnesses, however, the Iron Curtain has faded away like a bad dream; to many among the younger generations, it remains an enduring mystery.

---

[183] Roman Grafe, *Deutsche Gerechtigkeit* (Siedler, 2004).
[184] *TAZ*, 11/3/1993, p. 8; *NZZ*, 2/19/1997, p. 5.
[185] *DPA*, 6/20/2023, https://proxy.library.mcgill.ca/login?url=https://www.proquest.com/wire-feeds/toteam-eisernen-vorhang-angeklagter-ex-minister/docview/2827729733/se-2?accountid=12339, accessed on July 30, 2025.
[186] See various articles in: Meinke, *Die tschechisch-bayerische Grenze*.

Primary Sources Used

Archives

Germany, Berlin Lichterfelde, *Bundesarchiv* [Bundesarchiv Lichterfelde]
Germany, Berlin, *Landesarchiv* [Landesarchiv Berlin]
Germany, Freiburg, *Bundesarchiv* [Bundesarchiv Freiburg]
United States, CIA, *Freedom of Information Act Electronic Reading Room* [FOIA Reading Room]. www.cia.gov/readingroom/home, accessed in January and February 2025

Newspapers

Note: morning/noon/evening editions are marked with an -m/-n/-e after the title of the newspapers, f.e.: *NZZ*-m is the morning edition of the *Neue Zürcher Zeitung*.

Berner Tagwacht [BT]
Bieler Tagblatt
Boston Globe [BG]
Chicago Daily Tribune [CDT]
Chicago Tribune [CT]
China Press [CP]
China Weekly Review [CWR]
Daily Boston Globe [DBG]
Der Bund [Bund]
Deutsche Depeschen Agentur [DPA]
Die Tat [Tat]
Die Tageszeitung [TAZ]
Freiburger Nachrichten
Hamilton Spectator [HS]
Hindustan Times [HT]
Jerusalem Post [JP]
Jewish Exponent [JE]
Manchester Guardian [MG]
Neue Zürcher Nachrichten [NZN]
Neue Zürcher Zeitung [NZZ]
Nevada State Journal [NSJ]
New York Times [NYT]

New York Tribune [NYTribune]
Newsweek
Observer
Palestine Post [PP]
Scotsman
South China Morning Post [SCMP]
The Austin American [AA]
The Austin Statesman [AS]
The Calgary Daily Herald [CDH]
The Christian Science Monitor [CSM]
The Globe and Mail [GM]
The Guardian
The Hartford Courant [HC]
The Irish Times [IT]
The Sun
The Washington Post [WP]

Note on Terminology

A *border strip* refers to the access-prohibited belt of land up to 20 meters wide and directly adjacent to the actual border line. It often contained a border fence or wall, a path/street for regular border guard patrols, and sometimes electrical fences and/or minefields.

A *border zone* refers to an adjacent belt up to circa 500 meters wide. Often, it was cleared of vegetation and buildings, sometimes contained minefields, customarily was access-restricted or access-prohibited, and often was depopulated. In a few cases, the zone reached up to 2,000 meters inland.

A *border area* refers to an access-controlled belt adjacent to the border zone and measuring up to circa 15 kilometers (sometimes even more) into the interior. Suspect residents or even all populations were forcibly removed from this area; in some cases, buildings were destroyed.

A *border region* refers to a belt adjacent to the border area and reaching up to several tens of kilometers into the hinterland. Here, police or secret police surveilled movement of people, denied access, or arrested potential and suspected escapees.

The terms *boundary* and *border* are used interchangeably.

Further Readings

Bencsik, Péter, and Nagy György. *A magyar úti okmányok története 1945–89* [History of Hungarian Travel Documents 1945–1989]. Tipico Design Kft., 2005.

Dullin, Sabine. *La frontière épaisse: aux origines des politiques soviétiques (1920–1940)* [The Thick Border: The Origins of Soviet Policies (1920–1940)]. EHESS, 2014.

Flemming, Thomas. *Die Berliner Mauer: Geschichte eines politischen Bauwerks* [The Berlin Wall: History of a Political Edifice]. Bundeszentrale für politische Bildung, 2019.

Frey, Felix. "A Fluid Iron Curtain: Norwegian–Soviet Hydropower Cooperation in the Pasvik Valley, 1955–1965," *Scandinavian Journal of History*, 45/4 (2020), pp. 506–26.

Harrison, Hope M. *Driving the Soviets up the Wall: Soviet-East German Relations, 1953–1961*. Princeton University Press, 2011.

Heeresgeschichtliches Museum Wien. *Der Eiserne Vorhang* [The Iron Curtain]. Heeresgeschichtliches Museum, 2001.

Kim Hyung-geun. *The DMZ: Dividing the Two Koreas*. Korea Foundation, 2010.

Lohr, Eric. *Soviet Citizenship: From Empire to Soviet Union*. Harvard University Press, 2012.

Meinke, Markus A. *Die tschechisch-bayerische Grenze im Kalten Krieg in vergleichender Perspektive* [The Czech-Bavarian border in the Cold War in a comparative perspective]. Stadtarchiv Regensburg, 2011.

Nunan, Timothy. "The Violence Curtain: Occupied Afghan Turkestan & the Making of a Central Asian Borderscape," *Transcultural Studies*, 8/1 (2017), pp. 224–58.

Rottman, Gordon L., and Chris Taylor. *The Berlin Wall and the Inner-German Border 1961–89*. Osprey, 2008.

Rychlík, Jan. *Cestování do ciziny v habsburské monarchii a v Ceskoslovensku* [Traveling abroad in the Habsburg Monarchy and Czechoslovakia]. Ústav pro soudobé dějiny AV ČR, 2007.

Sälter, Gerhard. *Das Grenzregime im Zentrum Berlins* [The border regime in the center of Berlin]. Ch. Links, 2018.

Scott, Erik R. *Defectors: How the Illicit Flight of Soviet Citizens Built the Borders of the Cold War World*. Oxford University Press, 2023.

Taylor, Frederick. *The Berlin Wall: A World Divided*. HarperCollins, 2006.

Technical Museum Brno, ed. *Der Eiserne Vorhang, 1948–1989* [The Iron Curtain, 1948–1989]. Technické muzeum, 2019.

Acknowledgments

As with so many projects, this one too would not have seen the day of the light without the help of friends, colleagues, and librarians. Devoid of any considerations regarding order, I am grateful for the advice, tips, help, and references from Kristy Ironside, Mark Edele, Andrey Shlyakhter, Tara Zahra, László Borhi, Louis Clerc, Judith Szapor, Maria Popova, Elidor Mëhilli, Juliet Johnson, Piotr H. Kosicki, Jens Schöne, Laura Madokoro, Maximilian Graf, Sabina Ferhadbegović, and Gerhard Sälter. Also, many thanks to the librarians at McGill, who fulfilled many of my extravagant interlibrary loan requests. I am grateful for Ruilan Shi for producing Maps 2, 3, 6, 7, 11, and 12. A big thank you goes to Donnie Morard for carefully proofreading the manuscript twice. Finally, I would like to express my appreciation to the two Elements Series editors Rebecca Friedman and Mark Edele, the CUP editors Liz Friend-Smith and Julia Ford, and two anonymous reviewers who provided detailed and concise feedback and criticism.

Funds from Canada's Social Sciences and Humanities Research Council [435–2023-0395] were used for the purchase of copyrights and the production of maps.

I dedicate this short volume to my students whose excellent questions have spurred me to rethink many of my views about the Cold War over two decades. In recent years, I realized that they don't have an intuitive understanding of the Iron Curtain, which I, as a European growing up in the late Cold War, always thought I had. I originally wrote this volume for them to understand, but ended up writing it also for myself in a process of rethinking what I believed I had already understood.

Disclaimer

The author made every effort to identify and contact the copyright holders and obtain permission for the use of all material in this work. Where this has not been possible, the author will be pleased to make any necessary corrections at the earliest opportunity.

Cambridge Elements

Soviet and Post-Soviet History

Mark Edele
University of Melbourne

Mark Edele teaches Soviet history at the University of Melbourne, where he is Hansen Professor in History. His most recent books are *Stalinism at War* (2021) and *Russia's War Against Ukraine* (2023). He is one of the convenors of the Research Initiative on Post-Soviet Space (RIPSS) at the University of Melbourne.

Rebecca Friedman
Florida International University

Rebecca Friedman is Founding Director of the Wolfsonian Public Humanities Lab and Professor of History at Florida International University in Miami. Her recent book, Modernity, Domesticity and Temporality: Time at Home, supported by the National Endowment for the Humanities, explores modern time and home in twentieth century Russia (2020). She is one of the editors for the Bloomsbury Academic series A Cultural History of Time.

About the Series

Elements in Soviet and Post-Soviet History pluralise the history of the former Soviet space. Contributions decolonise Soviet history and provincialise the former metropole: Russia. In doing so, the series provides an up-to-date history of the present of the region formerly known as the Soviet Union.

Cambridge Elements

Soviet and Post-Soviet History

Elements in the Series

Making National Diasporas: Soviet-Era Migrations and Post-Soviet Consequences
Lewis H. Siegelbaum and Leslie Page Moch

Ukraine not 'the' Ukraine
Marta Dyczok

The Fate of the Soviet Bloc's Military Alliance: Reform, Adaptation, and Collapse of the Warsaw Pact, 1985–1991
Mark Kramer

Central Asia – Russia's Near Abroad or Crossroads of Asia?
Richard Pomfret

Environment and Society in Soviet Estonia, 1960–1990: An Intimate Cultural History an Intimate Cultural History
Epp Annus

Ukrainian Literature: A Wartime Guide for Anglophone Readers
Marko Pavlyshyn

Decolonizing Russia?: Disentangling Debates
Adam Lenton et al.

The Iron Curtain: A Short History of Socialist Borders
Lorenz M. Lüthi

A full series listing is available at: www.cambridge.org/ESPH

For EU product safety concerns, contact us at Calle de José Abascal, 56–1°,
28003 Madrid, Spain or eugpsr@cambridge.org.

www.ingramcontent.com/pod-product-compliance
Lightning Source LLC
LaVergne TN
LVHW011854060526
838200LV00054B/4323